ANCIENT FOREST FRIENDLY

17 trees were saved for our forests

Preserving our environment

Indigo Books.Gifts.Life chose to use recycled paper for all print editions of this book and saved these resources[1]:

energy	water	greenhouse gases	solid waste
7 million BTUs	28,860 L	55 kg	117 kg

Printed by **Webcom Inc.**
on Legacy Book Opaque 100% post-consumer waste.

FSC
Recycled
Supporting responsible use of forest resources
Cert no. SW-COC-002358
www.fsc.org
© 1996 Forest Stewardship Council

[1]Estimates were made using the Environmental Defense Paper Calculator.

Manufacturing this book in Canada ensures compliance with strict environmental practices and eliminates the need for international freight, which is a major contributor to global air pollution

Statistics & Data Analysis

COLES NOTES STUDY GUIDE

ABOUT COLES NOTES

COLES NOTES have been an indispensible aid to students on five continents since 1948.

COLES NOTES are available for a wide range of individual literary works. Clear, concise explanations and insights are provided along with interesting interpretations and evaluations.

Proper use of COLES NOTES will allow the student to pay greater attention to lectures and spend less time taking notes. This will result in a broader understanding of the work being studied and will free the student for increased participation in discussions.

COLES NOTES are an invaluable aid for review and exam preparation as well as an invitation to explore different interpretive paths.

COLES NOTES are written by experts in their fields. It should be noted that any literary judgement expressed herein is just that - the judgement of one school of thought. Interpretations that diverge from, or totally disagree with any criticism may be equally valid.

COLES NOTES are designed to supplement the text and are not intended as a substitute for reading the text itself. Use of the NOTES will serve not only to clarify the work being studied, but should enhance the readers enjoyment of the topic.

ISBN 978-1-5526-7795-7

Coles Publishing
A division of Prospero Books
Toronto Canada
Publisher: Indigo Books and Music Inc.

Designed and Printed in Canada

Printed on Legacy Book Opaque 100%, manufactured from 100% post-consumer waste and is FSC-certified. Manufacturing this book in Canada ensures compliance with strict environmental practices and eliminates the need for international freight shipping, a major contributor to global air pollution.

Manufactured by Webcom

Contents

Statistics and data analysis

Introduction

Statistics is a branch of mathematics that deals with collecting, organizing, displaying and analyzing data. The information obtained is used to make predictions and decisions in many different situations.

Consider these statements:

- A new passive security device for cars resulted in a 77% reduction in theft.
- The opening-day crowd of 31 227 was 400 below the average for last season.
- Heart disease is the leading cause of death among Canadians.
- There is a significant positive correlation between education level and income.
- Statistics show that there is a need to build an additional runway at the airport.

In order to understand the exact meaning of these statements and to judge their validity, you need to learn the methods and vocabulary of statistics and data collection.

Statistical knowledge will help you analyze issues in the news and it may also be important in your career. Statisticians collect and interpret data, and people in many other fields make use of statistics in their work. A doctor determines if a baby is growing normally by comparing the baby's height and weight to a table of heights and weights of healthy infants. A financial counselor makes a decision about which investment to recommend by studying data on the yearly returns and market behavior of many companies. Engineers building a bridge analyze traffic pattern statistics for the surrounding area. Forecasters predict the strength of a hurricane by examining the data on past hurricanes. Car manufacturers use data on leg-length and arm-reach to design cars with pedals and knobs that are accessible to most drivers. No matter which career you choose, an understanding of statistical basics will be important.

Other Coles Notes covering topics in senior mathematics:

Topics in senior math are frequently interconnected at each grade level. These additional titles from Coles Notes will help you master them all:

How to Get an A in ...

- Permutations and Combinations
- Senior Algebra
- Sequences and Series
- Trigonometry and Circle Geometry
- Calculus

CHAPTER ONE

Data collection

DATA

The first step in the statistical process is the collection of data. *Data* is the information gathered for a study. It can be obtained through:

- surveys, questionnaires or interviews
- observations
- experiments or simulations
- books, newspapers or databases

Usually data is collected from a sample of the population.

> The **population** is the whole group of people or things that is being studied. A **sample** is the part of the population on which information will actually be collected. A sample is used when it is too time-consuming, expensive or destructive to survey the entire population. The results are then used to make predictions about the entire population.

Example 1

Martha wants to know how many 14-year-old girls in Canada are over 150 cm tall. How can she arrive at an estimate?

It would take too long for Martha to measure all Canadian 14-year-old girls. She chooses a sample of 50 14-year-old girls and uses her data to predict the results for the whole population. If 25 of the girls in Martha's sample are over 150 cm, then she would conclude that 50% of Canadian 14-year-old girls are taller than 150 cm.

Example 2

Ace Importing wants to run a quality-control test on its shipment of Giant Spiral Fireworks. There are 50 boxes of 100 Giant Spirals. How should it conduct the testing?

If all 5 000 fireworks were tested, there would be none left to sell. Therefore, the staff at Ace decides to test one per box and make a decision about quality from this sample of 50. If 5 of the 50 Giant Spirals in the sample fizzle out, then 10% of the sample is defective. Ace would then conclude that 10% of the whole shipment is defective.

Sometimes a sample in one study is the population in another. For instance, Ted wants to know how many students at Fieldcrest School own a computer. A **sample** for his study is the students in Mr. Smith's math class at Fieldcrest School. Brian wants to know how many students in Mr. Smith's math class at Fieldcrest School own a computer. The **population** of his study is the students in Mr. Smith's math class at Fieldcrest School.

RANDOM SAMPLE

In order to make accurate predictions from any sample, we must make sure it *is* a random sample. A **random sample** is a sample selected in such a way that every member of the population involved has an equal chance of being included. Drawing names from a hat or picking every third name in the phone book are two ways of selecting a random sample.

Example 3

Joanne wants to estimate the number of students at Simpson High who have a driver's license. There are over 1000 students and she has decided to interview 30. How should she choose her sample?

The population of Joanne's study is all the students at

Simpson High. *Therefore, all the students at Simpson High should have an equal chance of being included. Joanne can choose a random sample by drawing 30 names from a hat containing the names of all the students in the school.*

If Joanne surveys only her grade 12 math class, no student from grades 9, 10 or 11 has a chance of being included. Thus the sample will not represent all the students at Simpson High. Joanne's data will be *biased* because it will not include results from the junior students who are too young to drive. Her estimate of the number of drivers will be too high.

TABLE OF RANDOM DIGITS

One method of choosing a random sample is to use a table of random digits.

A **table of random digits** is a table of numbers in columns. In practice, tables are produced by having a computer generate random digits, but you can easily produce a table of random one-digit numbers. Put tags with the numbers 0 to 9 in a box. Draw a tag, write its number in the table, replace the tag and repeat the procedure.

Example 4

From a list of 40 households, 5 are to be surveyed about the brand of toothpaste they use.

a) Use a table of random digits to select the households to be surveyed.

b) Use the random feature on a calculator to select the households.

a) *Assign each household a number between 0 and 39. In a table of random two-digit numbers, circle each number that corresponds to a household until you have selected 5. For example, in the table below, households 5, 23, 18, 2 and 12 would be surveyed.*

64	76	90	(05)	82	(23)	41	(18)	57
80	99	45	67	(02)	95	54	88	(12)

b) *Many scientific calculators generate random numbers. Look for the word* **random** *or the abbreviation* **rand** *on your calculator. Usually this function will produce a three-digit number between 0 and 1. Therefore, assign each household a number between 0.000 and 0.039. Household number 25 would be assigned number 0.025. Then use the random feature to create a list of numbers:*

0.928 0.799 (0.006) 0.790 0.519 0.106 0.042 0.112 (0.030) (0.017) (0.035) 0.185 0.772 (0.026) 0.000 0.223 0.534 0.680

Based on this list, households numbered 6, 30, 17, 35 and 26 would be surveyed.

Your table or calculator may give longer or shorter random numbers.

You can ignore extra digits: 0.3256221 can represent 0.3256 or 0.325.

If you need more digits, you can put two numbers together: 652 163 can represent 652163 or 6521.

CONDUCTING SIMULATIONS

Sometimes we would like to collect data on a problem, but it is too time-consuming or difficult to use a survey or carry out an experiment. We can simulate the results by carrying out an experiment that has the same probability.

Example 5

Paula wants to know how frequently triplets are all girls. What can she use in a simulation that will have the same probability as this event?

Paula knows that the probability of having a girl is 1/2. The probability of getting a head with a coin is also 1/2, so she can use three tosses of a coin to simulate the birth of triplets. Every time she gets three heads in a row, she has simulated the birth of an all-girl set of triplets.

Example 6

The student council is running a school carwash to raise money. The students hope to attract 30 cars in 6 hours. Three students can wash one car in 10 minutes. Geoff, the council president, wants to work out how many students to schedule to avoid lineups. How can he use a simulation to help?

It would appear at first that Geoff can run the carwash with just three students because 30 cars in 6 hours is 1 car every 12 minutes, which allows time for washing. However, cars may not arrive exactly at 12-minute intervals. Geoff can simulate the scenario by using a spinner that has the same probability as the car arrivals. He divides a spinner into 12 numbered sections and chooses the number 5 to represent the arrival of a car. He spins 30 times to simulate 30 minutes and records his results:

1	**2**	**3**	**4**	**5**	**6**	**7**	**8**	**9**	**10**	**11**	**12**	**13**	**14**	**15**
6	10	2	5	3	3	9	8	1	9	5	4	7	2	11
16	**17**	**18**	**19**	**20**	**21**	**22**	**23**	**24**	**25**	**26**	**27**	**28**	**29**	**30**
1	11	6	5	3	12	5	4	1	3	7	6	10	1	12

The "cars" arrive at minutes 4, 11, 19 and 22. In this simulation, there isn't time to finish washing each car before another arrives. The second car will have to wait 3 minutes in line. The third car will have to wait 4 minutes. The fourth car will arrive before the students start washing the third car! From this brief experiment, Geoff learns that he will need two teams of students to handle the carwash.

Simulations are frequently carried out using computer programs. Geoff can run a full simulation of the entire 6 hours in just a few moments using a spreadsheet. See chapter 8 for an example.

TALLY CHARTS

The word *tally* means *count*. When data is collected, it is often recorded in a *tally chart* to keep track of the totals.

Example 6

Joyce is surveying students at lunch to find out which foods in the cafeteria are most popular. How should she set up her tally chart?

The first column lists the foods Joyce is asking about. The second column is for check marks. The third column is called

Frequency and is the place to record the total number of check marks. Joyce's tally chart might look like this:

Choices	Tally	Frequency
Hamburger	✓ ✓ ✓ ✓ ✓ ✓ ✓ ✓ ✓ ✓ ✓ ✓ ✓ ✓ ✓	15
Pizza	✓ ✓ ✓ ✓ ✓ ✓ ✓ ✓ ✓	9
Soup & sandwich	✓ ✓ ✓ ✓ ✓ ✓ ✓ ✓ ✓ ✓ ✓ ✓	12
Chicken fingers	✓ ✓ ✓ ✓ ✓ ✓	6

***Example** 7*

Bill and Sarah have also done a survey in the lunchroom. How can they link their information with Joyce's and make predictions to effectively order the most popular foods?

The data from the three tally charts can be put together and percentages calculated:

	Joyce	Bill	Sarah	Totals	Ratio	Percentage
Hamburgers	15	12	21	48	$\frac{48}{128}$	37.5%
Pizza	9	18	13	40	$\frac{40}{128}$	31.25%
Soup & sandwich	12	8	4	24	$\frac{24}{128}$	18.75%
Chicken fingers	6	3	7	16	$\frac{16}{128}$	12.5%
Totals	42	41	45	128	$\frac{128}{128}$	100%

From this chart the students notice that hamburgers and pizza are the most popular foods in the cafeteria. Since 37.5% of their survey group liked hamburgers, they could predict that out of 1200 students at the school, 37.5% or 450 prefer the cafeteria hamburgers.

To calculate a percent from a ratio:

$\frac{48}{128} \rightarrow 48 \div 128 \times 100 = 37.5\%$

To calculate a percent of a total:

37.5% of $1200 \rightarrow 1200 \times 0.375 = 450$

PRACTICE EXERCISE

1. Describe how you would gather data to support the following statements:
   a) A new passive security device for cars resulted in a 77% reduction in theft.
   b) The opening-day crowd of 31 227 was 400 below the average for last season.
   c) Statistics show that there is a need to build an additional runway at the airport.

2. Why is it important when gathering data to select a random sample of the population?

3. Melanie wants to estimate the number of students at her school who have part-time jobs. There are over 1000 students and she has decided to interview 40. Describe how she could choose her sample.

4. Jacques was hired to conduct a survey on traffic concerns in a neighborhood consisting of 400 households. Describe how Jacques can select a random sample of 50 households:
   a) using a table of random digits
   b) using the random feature on a calculator

5. Leila wants to know how common it is that all 4 children in a family have birthdays in the same month.
   a) What can she use in a simulation that will have the same probability as this event?
   b) Describe how she would carry out the simulation.

6. The following information was gathered from 50 community-college students in a survey to investigate the number of hours worked at part-time jobs.
   - 16 students did not work
   - 10 students worked less than 5 hours a week
   - 14 students worked between 5 and 10 hours a week
   - 8 students worked between 10 and 15 hours a week
   - 2 students worked more than 15 hours a week

   a) Set up a tally sheet to display the information.
   b) Calculate the percentage of students in each category.
   c) Based on this study predict the number of students in a group of 300 000 who would work more than 15 hours a week.

CHAPTER TWO

Presentation of data

The second step in the statistical process is the presentation of data in a format that will help us to notice important features and communicate our findings.

FREQUENCY DISTRIBUTIONS AND HISTOGRAMS

After data is collected it is often organized in a frequency table and then displayed in a histogram to make it easier to observe any patterns.

Example 1

A survey of 50 grade 12 students to find the length of time spent each day watching television produced the following results:

2	3	1	1	1	3	4	2	5	2	3	3	2	4	3	1	2	3	2	4	1	1	6	1	2
1	4	3	4	2	5	3	1	2	3	2	4	2	1	1	3	2	2	2	1	4	3	2	3	2

Organize this data in a frequency table and display it in a histogram.

The students watched between 1 and 6 hours of TV so the first column represents the hours. As each 1 in the table above is counted, a stroke is marked in the Tally column and then the total written in the Frequency column. This procedure is repeated for the other hours.

Hours	Tally	Frequency
1	𝍸 𝍸 𝍷𝍷	12
2	𝍸 𝍸 𝍸 𝍷	16
3	𝍸 𝍸 𝍷𝍷	12
4	𝍸 𝍷𝍷	7
5	𝍷𝍷	2
6	𝍷	1

It is now clear that most of the surveyed students watch between 1 and 3 hours of TV a day.

Another way to display the data is with a histogram. It is easy to see from this histogram that the most common number of hours of TV watching is 2.

The bar at 6 hours is very small because only 1 student admitted that he watches 6 hours of TV a day.

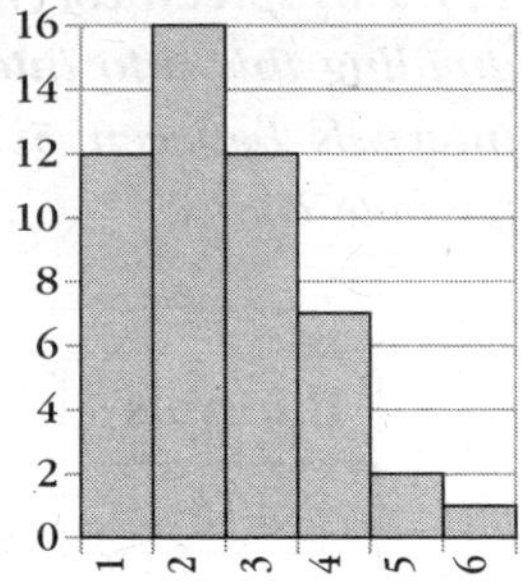

Often there is a wide range of numbers in the data collected and it would be confusing to represent each number separately. In this case, data is grouped and then displayed.

When grouping data, keep these points in mind:

- Choose intervals that are the same length.
- Try to keep the number of intervals between 5 and 20. Too many are confusing and too few do not illustrate the data clearly.
- There should be no gaps between intervals.

Example 2

Ron is helping the children at Camp Pineview find out how far a turtle travels in half an hour. He and the children record the distances travelled by 50 turtles, round the results to the nearest centimetre and record them as follows:

2	82	64	73	89	38	55	99	63	25
48	106	33	27	54	61	114	60	58	51
21	51	41	93	53	11	15	39	86	66
121	49	75	46	29	71	26	19	73	53
35	23	97	84	56	75	60	59	32	46

Display this data in a frequency table and in a histogram.

The smallest number in Ron's data is 2 and the largest is 121. This spread covers 120 numbers. There are many options for dividing this into intervals but we want to keep the number of intervals between 5 and 20. Using 10 intervals of 12 is one possible choice.

Intervals	Tally	Frequency
2-14	||	2
14-26	𝍸	5
26-38	𝍸 |	6
38-50	𝍸 ||	7
50-62	𝍸 𝍸 ||	12
62-74	𝍸 |	6
74-86	||||	4
86-98	||||	4
98-110	||	2
110-122	||	2

If a number occurs on a boundary, it belongs to the upper group. That is, 14 belongs in the 14-26 group. Sometimes this is shown by writing [2-14) and [14-26). The square bracket means that the number next to it is included in the interval.

An alternate way to design intervals is to use decimals. In displaying Ron's data we could use the intervals (1.5-13.5), (13.5-25.5), (25.5-37.5), up to (109.5-121.5). This method ensures that whole number data never occurs on a boundary.

In this histogram the most common distance for a turtle to cover was 56 cm in half an hour, but 2 turtles hardly moved at all while several turtles travelled over 1 metre.

When drawing a histogram, use the middle number of the interval to label the horizontal axis. Do not leave gaps between the bars of the histogram.

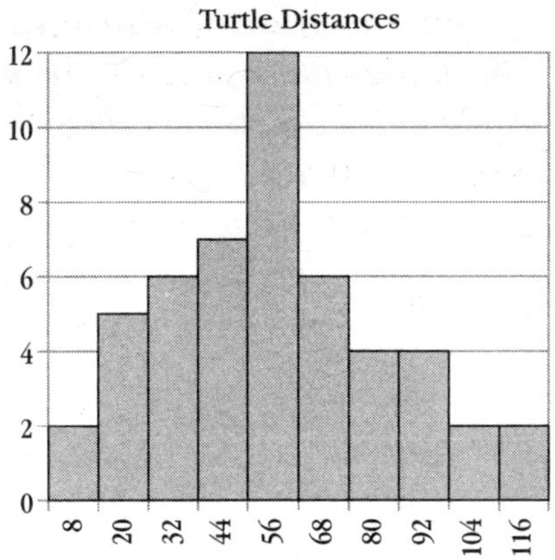

GRAPHICAL REPRESENTATIONS OF DATA

Circle graphs, broken line graphs, bar graphs and pictographs can all be used to illustrate data, but it is important to choose the type of graph that will best explain the results.

Usually:

- Circle graphs are used to illustrate how something is broken into parts.
- Broken line graphs are used to show how something changes over time.
- Bar graphs are used to compare things that are alike.
- Pictographs are used to attract the reader by presenting information visually.

Example 3

Choose the type of graph that will illustrate each of the following situations best:

a) how the government spends $1.00 of tax revenue

b) Canada's exports

c) the heights of the mountains of North America

d) the value of the Canadian dollar over a 20-year period

a) *The government will divide the $1.00 among various initiatives. A circle graph will give a clear picture of the fraction that is spent on the environment, defense and so on.*

b) *This could be displayed using a pictograph. Sheaves of wheat and illustrations of computer terminals, for example, would provide a strong visual image of the relationships between exports of agricultural and high-tech products.*

c) *A bar graph will illustrate this data very well.*

d) *To appreciate the changing nature of the value of the dollar over this period, the best representation would be a broken line graph.*

Example 4

Joan spends her day as shown in the chart. Draw a graph to illustrate this information.

Sleep	10 hours
School	6 hours
Eating	2 hour
Sports	3 hours
Homework	2 hours
Relaxation	1 hour

Since this information shows how something is divided, it should be illustrated with a circle graph.

The sections of a circle graph must correspond to the proportions in the data. If one-quarter of Joan's day is spent at school, then one-quarter of the circle should represent school.

To draw the circle graph for Joan's day:

- *Find the percentage of time spent on a particular activity.*
- *Use the percentage to find the number of degrees in that section of the circle.*
- *Draw a circle and measure the angles with a protractor.*
- *Label the sections with the names of the activities and the percentage.*

Activity	Hours	Percentage Divide the hours by 24 and multiply by 100		Degrees Multiply the percentage by 360°
Sleep	10	$\frac{10}{24} = 0.4167$	41.7%	360 × 41.7% = 150°
School	6	$\frac{6}{24} = 0.25$	25%	360 × 25% = 90°
Eating	2	$\frac{2}{24} = 0.083$	8.3%	360 × 8.3% = 30°
Sports	3	$\frac{3}{24} = 0.125$	12.5%	360 × 12.5% = 45°
Homework	2	$\frac{2}{24} = 0.083$	8.3%	360 × 8.3% = 30°
Relaxation	1	$\frac{1}{24} = 0.042$	4.2%	360 × 4.2% = 15°

The percentage column must add up to 100% and the degree column must total 360°. Check before drawing your graph

Joan's Day

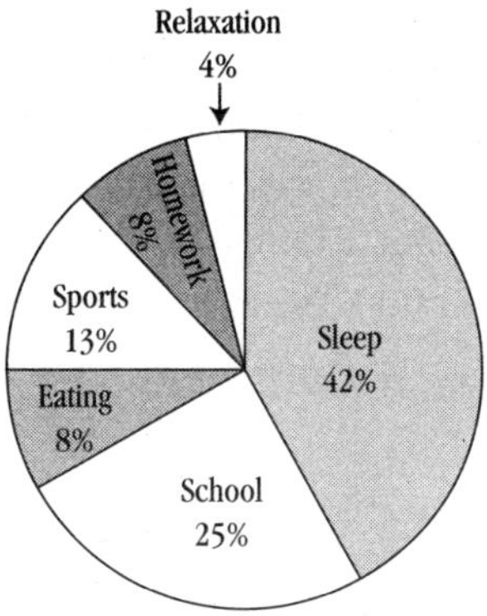

Always include a title, the section name and the percentage in your graph. If the graph has very small sections you can use an arrow to show where the label belongs.

When calculating the degrees for a section of a circle graph, reduce round-off errors by doing all steps without clearing your calculator. Try this experiment.

Step #1 Enter 10 ÷ 24 on your calculator. You should get 0.41666...

Now multiply 360 by 41.7%. Your calculator will read 150.12.

Step #2 Enter 10 ÷ 24 on your calculator. You should get 0.41666...

Now enter × 360. Your calculator should read 150.

The error in the 150.12 is caused by rounding the percentage to 41.7. Leaving the number on the screen lets the calculator use the entire value and gives the correct answer of 150.

MISLEADING STATISTICS

Graphs and charts frequently accompany articles in newspapers and magazines and are often used in advertising brochures. As consumers we should examine these carefully because data displays and pseudo-statistics can be misleading.

Example 5

Tenstar Computers is putting out an advertising brochure to show the company's sales figures over the past 4 years. Their gross earnings in 1996 were $400 000; in 1997, $450 000; in 1998, $520 000; and in 1999, $600 000. Examine their graph and explain why it is misleading.

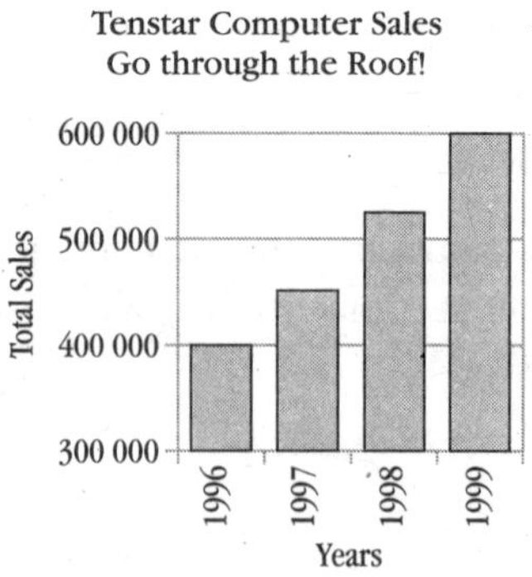

In Tenstar's advertising graph, the vertical axis starts at $300 000 instead of 0. Although the data is correctly plotted, this alteration in the vertical axis makes it appear that Tenstar has been growing at a very fast rate. Tenstar's true growth can be seen in the next graph.

This bar graph shows the true picture of Tenstar Computers. They have been experiencing moderate growth, not the spectacular growth shown in their brochure graph.

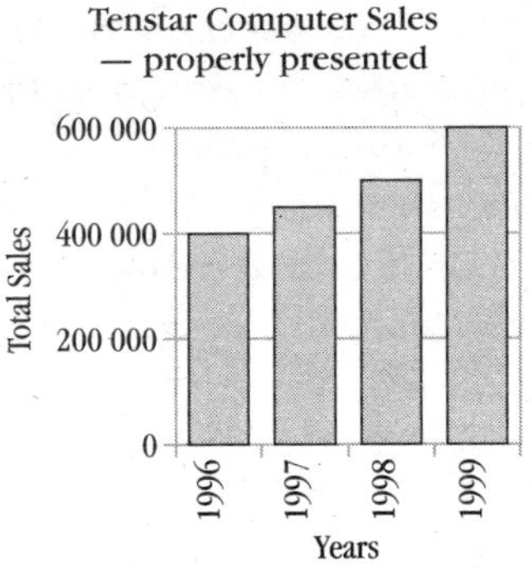

Example 6

What erroneous conclusions might be drawn from the following?

An insurance brochure states that 80% of all car accidents happen within 2 kilometres of home.

It might be tempting to conclude from this statement that people should only drive when far away from their houses, or that it's safer to drive on the highway than in the city or town. However, if statistics showed that 80% of all driving is done within 2 kilometres of home we might reasonably predict that 80% of all accidents should happen within 2 kilometres of home.

COMPARING GRAPHS

Sometimes it is helpful to view two graphs on the same axes in order to compare them.

Example 7

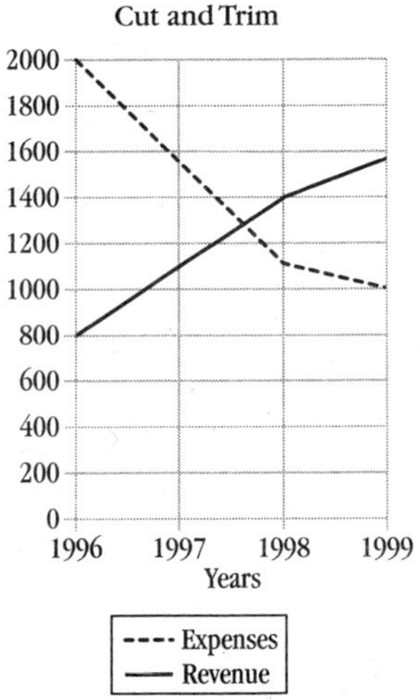

Jon and Brian started their student business, Cut and Trim Lawn Care, three years ago. They plotted their expenses and revenue on the same axes. How can this graph help them to analyze their financial position?

The graph shows that Jon and Brian's expenses started high at $2000 but have come down and are now starting to level off at about $1000 per year.

Their revenue for the first year was low, at $800, but has gone up each year, and this year they brought in almost $1600.

Jon and Brian can also see where the revenue line and the expense line cross. This is called the break-even point. It is the point where revenues and expenses are the same; that is, when the amount earned is equal to the amount spent. In 1998 revenues were more than expenses so their business earned a profit that year.

> When you put two graphs on the same axes, make sure to use the same scale for both sets of data. Use different colours or line qualities to differentiate between the graphs.

STEM AND LEAF PLOTS

A stem and leaf plot looks like a histogram on its side, but it includes the original data instead of counting it.

Example 8

The manager of Bruner's Deli Counter decided to save time by offering prepackaged slabs of cheddar cheese. In order to stock the counter with the most popular sizes, he recorded the weights (in g) of the amounts his customers bought for two weeks.

268	320	335	310	320	260	255	275	305	255
320	325	250	266	325	350	325	250	310	320
250	250	290	284	270	320	260	280	325	255

Display this data using a stem and leaf plot. Then explain how this illustration can help the manager.

> In a stem and leaf plot, the first part of the number is the stem and the second part is the leaf. For example:
>
> - 32 could be written with 3 as the stem and 2 as the leaf
> - 48.6 could be written with 48 as the stem and 6 as the leaf

In the data from Bruner's Deli Counter, we can use the first two digits as the stem and the third as the leaf. The "stems" are then 25, 26, 27 and so on, up to 35. They are written in a column. The first number, 268, has 8 as its leaf so 8 is written beside 26 in the right-hand column. When another number starting with 26 is found, its leaf is written beside 8 with no comma.

From the plot, the manager can see that in the past two weeks he sold cheddar in 250 to 350 g packages.

He can also notice that most customers prefer packages around 250 g and 320 g.

This information will help him decide how large the prewrapped packages should be and how many he should provide of each size.

25	0 0 0 5 0 5 5
26	8 6 0 0
27	0 5
28	4 0
29	0
30	5
31	0 0
32	0 0 5 0 5 0 5 5 0
33	5
34	
35	0

PRACTICE EXERCISE

1. A survey of 30 car owners calculating the number of kilometres travelled in one week, produced the following results (rounded to the nearest km):

200	330	305	242	251	334	238	321	382	449	299	358	399	423	413
226	300	364	325	314	263	419	281	338	322	378	295	347	327	276

a) Organize this data in a frequency table.

b) Display it in a histogram.

2. Choose the type of graph that will illustrate each of the following situations best:

a) how a typical teenager budgets money

b) the types of pets owned by Canadians

c) the change in the population of caribou over the past 50 years

d) densities of different types of wood

3. A college brochure sets out estimates of costs for first year. They suggest the following amounts (see box).

Draw a circle graph to illustrate this information.

Tuition	$4150
Books	$550
Internet Fee	$50
Residence (including food)	$4600
Personal	$450
Transportation	$200

4. Explain why this graph of the sales of Nostar Motors is misleading.

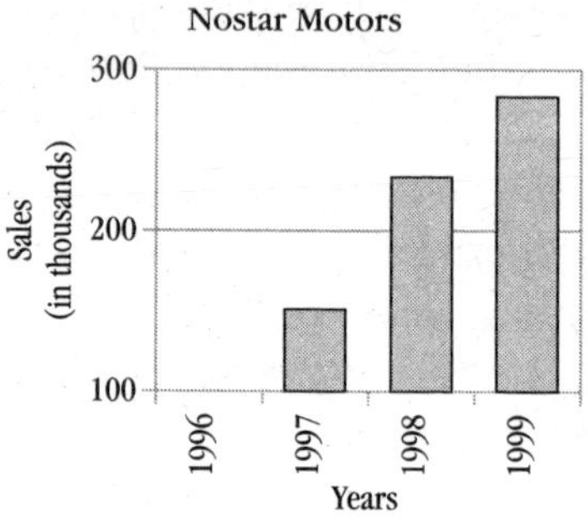

5. Green's Audio and Video gathered the following data on sales of tapes and CD's last year. Plot the information on the same graph and suggest how the owner could use this to make decisions for next year.

Sales (in thousands of dollars)

	Jan	Feb	Mar	Apr	May	Jun	Jul	Aug	Sep	Oct	Nov	Dec
Tapes	28	26	18	15	14	13.5	12	11.5	11	10	7	5
CD's	10	14	16.5	18	20	21	24	27	28	31	32	34

6. The following chart records the percentages received by 24 students on a geometry test. Display this data using a stem and leaf plot.

63	47	92	66	84	85	74	75	71	85	60	83
68	77	79	90	53	73	57	65	88	77	86	98

CHAPTER THREE

Measures of central tendency

When data is displayed in a graph or chart, it is often possible to notice general trends. But there are additional tools to analyze data that can give us more information.

The mean, median and mode are three measures of central tendency. They help us locate the center of the data, and this allows us to make predictions about what is "likely" to happen.

- The **arithmetic mean** is often called the average.
- The **median** is the middle number in an ordered list of data.
- The **mode** is the most common number.

MEAN

Most students have learned that to find the mean (or average) of 10 numbers, you should add all the numbers and then divide by 10. But it is important in statistics to understand why this works and what the mean can tell us about data.

Example 1

Pat got 75%, 80% and 88% on three tests. Find his average without a formula.

Think of making all three marks the same. Take 5 marks from the highest test and add it to the lowest. Pat now has 80%, 80% and 83%. Now take 2 marks from the 83% and give 1 to each of the other marks. That leaves 81%, 81% and 81%. Pat's average is 81%. Notice that Pat still has a total of 243 marks. They are just redistributed into 3 even groups. Notice also that Pat's average is between his lowest and highest marks.

- The mean of a set of data is the value you would get if you took from the large numbers and gave to the small ones until all the numbers were the same.
- The mean of a set of data must lie between the lowest and highest numbers. The mean of 23, 44, 78, 35 and 42 must be a number between 23 and 78.

It is too difficult to find the average of a large set of data by the method of example 1 so we use a formula that finds the total and then uses division to split the data evenly into groups.

The simplest formula to find the mean of a *sample* of the population is:

$$\bar{x} = \frac{\Sigma x}{n}$$

- $\bar{x}$ (which is read x-bar) is the symbol for mean of a sample
- Σx is the sum of all the values in the sample
- n is the number of cases in the sample

Note: It is also possible to find the mean of the *population*, which is symbolized by the Greek letter μ (pronounce mu).

Example 2

Use the formula to find the mean of the following data:

45 63 52 85 37 81 55 34

Estimate first: The lowest value is 34 and the highest is 85, so our answer should be between these two numbers.

$\Sigma x = 45 + 63 + 52 + 85 + 37 + 81 + 55 + 34 = 452$

There are 8 numbers so $n = 8$.

$$\bar{x} = \frac{\Sigma x}{n} = \frac{452}{8} = 56.5$$

✓Check:

The mean value of 56.5 lies between 34 and 85.

8(56.5) = 452 The total of eight 56.5's is the same as the total of the original data.

Use your calculator to find the mean!
If your calculator has the symbols $\bar{x}$ and $\sum$+, or the words STAT or DATA, you can use it to find the mean. Look at the instruction book (if you kept it!), or try the following experiment.

Try typing 3, 18, 30 and either $\sum$ + or DATA after each number. Then press the $\bar{x}$ key. You should see 17, which is the mean of 3, 18 and 30.

Some calculators count the data as you enter it. Your calculator is one of these if it displayed 1 after you pressed 3, and 2 after you pressed 18.

To use the DATA button, you may need to put your calculator in STAT mode.

FINDING THE MEAN OF GROUPED DATA

A large amount of data is easier to handle when grouped. In this case, the mean can be calculated by the formula:

$$\bar{x} = \frac{\sum xf(x)}{n}$$

where $\sum xf(x)$ is the product of the different values and their frequencies.

Example 3

Mariette was canvassing for the Heart Fund and received the following amounts from 50 households. Find the average donation.

10	8	9	5	6	5	3	5	7	8
7	7	2	4	3	7	6	9	4	5
5	6	3	6	8	10	4	4	5	6
5	9	5	2	5	4	8	3	6	3
2	8	4	4	6	7	6	5	7	4

Organize the amounts into a frequency table:

Donation	Tally	Frequency
2	|||	3
3	~~||||~~	5
4	~~||||~~ |||	8
5	~~||||~~ ~~||||~~	10
6	~~||||~~ |||	8
7	~~||||~~ |	6
8	~~||||~~	5
9	|||	3
10	||	2

From the table we can see that 8 people donated $4 each. Therefore the frequency of 4 *is* 8 $\rightarrow f(4) = 8$.

$4 was donated by 8 people for a total of $32,
or: $4f(4) = 4(8) = 32$

To find the mean, enter the values and their frequencies in the formula.

$$
\begin{aligned}
\bar{x} &= \frac{\Sigma x f(x)}{n} \\
&= \frac{2f(2)+3f(3)+4f(4)+5f(5)+6f(6)+7f(7)+8f(8)+9f(9)+10f(10)}{50} \\
&= \frac{2(3)+3(5)+4(8)+5(10)+6(8)+7(6)+8(5)+9(3)+10(2)}{50} \\
&= \frac{6+15+32+50+48+42+40+27+20}{50} \\
&= \frac{280}{50} \\
&= 5.6
\end{aligned}
$$

Therefore the average donation was $5.60.

- **When working with groups of data, be careful to use the number of cases in the sample as the value for *n*. In the previous example, there were 9 groups but there were 50 contributors in the sample, so $n = 50$.**
- f (8) does not mean f multiplied by 8. It is the frequency, or number of times 8 appears in the data.

Sometimes data has been grouped into intervals. Finding the mean in these cases will only give an approximation of the true mean of the original data.

Example 4

The following chart summarizes the results of a rollerblade marathon for charity. Find the mean of the distances travelled by the participants.

Number of kilometres	Number of participants
0-5	20
5-10	35
10-15	42
15-20	38
20-25	15

Since the data has already been grouped, we don't know the make-up of the intervals. For example, there were 20 people who rollerbladed less than 5 kilometres. This could mean that 20 people rollerbladed 4 km each, or that 1 person went 4 km and 19 gave up at the starting line. To deal with this problem, we assume that everyone in a group rollerbladed the mean number of kilometres for that interval. Thus, for the first group we assume that all 20 people rollerbladed 2.5 km.

Use the formula for grouped data (don't forget there are 150 people!):

$$\bar{x} = \frac{\Sigma xf(x)}{n} = \frac{2.5(20)+7.5(35)+12.5(42)+17.5(38)+22.5(15)}{150}$$

$$= \frac{50+262.5+525+665+337.5}{150}$$

$$= \frac{1840}{150}$$

$$= 12.27$$

An approximation for the mean of this data is 12.27 km. We can say that the average distance travelled by the participants was about 12 km.

Calculating weighted means

When we calculate the mean, we usually try to make all values the same. However, sometimes it is important to give more weight to a particular value. Teachers do this when they weight the first term more heavily than the second term in the final mark.

Example 5

At Stormount High the final mark is calculated from 3 term marks, the first weighted at 60, the second at 100 and the third at 150. Find Janice's final mark if she received 83%, 68% and 71% in first, second and third term respectively.

The formula for a weighted mean is: $\bar{x} = \frac{\Sigma wx}{\Sigma w}$

where Σwx *is the sum of the data multiplied by their weightings and* Σw *is the sum of the weightings.*

Using the formula: $\frac{60(83)+100(68)+150(71)}{60+100+150} = \frac{22430}{310} = 72.35$

Therefore Janice's final mark is 72.4%. Calculated as a simple mean her average would have been 74%.

MEDIAN

The median, or middle value of an ordered list, is another important measure of central tendency. If George Fall earns the median salary of \$35 000 at Forest Plumbing, we know that half the people at the company earn more than George and half earn less.

To find the median:

- Organize the data from largest to smallest.
- If there is an odd number of values, the median is the middle value.
- If there is an even number of values, the median is the average of the two middle values.

Example 6

Find the median of the following sets of data:

a) marks of 7 students on a statistics quiz: 54, 79, 86, 90, 47, 73, 65

b) cost of room and board for 10 first-year college students: $5600, $6350, $4900, $7200, $4800, $6480, $4450, $5120, $4700, $6650

a) *Arrange the numbers from largest to smallest: 90, 86, 79, 73, 65, 54, 47. The middle number, 73, is the median. Half the numbers are smaller than 73 and half are larger.*

b) *Arrange the list of costs from largest to smallest: $7200, $6650, $6480, $6350, $5600, $5120, $4900, $4800, $4700, $4450*

In this list there is an even number of values. To find the median, take the average of the two middle values by adding them and dividing by 2.

$$\frac{5600+5120}{2}=5360$$

Therefore the median of the costs is $5360.

When a set of data is large, it is very time-consuming to list every value in order. A few simple techniques can make finding the median a little easier.

Example 7

Linke Office Management Systems has a president and 20 employees. The president earns $125 000. At the main office there is one financial officer who earns $85 000, one office manager at $75 000 and 4 clerical staff who earn $42 000 each. Six salespeople work from home for $61 000 each. Eight systems designers go out to work with clients and earn $80 000 apiece. Find the median salary at Linke.

Instead of listing the salaries of all 21 people in order, first organize them by groups from highest salary to lowest salary.

1 president	$125 000
1 financial officer	$85 000
8 systems designers	$80 000
1 office manager	$75 000
6 salespeople	$61 000
4 clerical staff	$42 000

Since there are 21 people, the 11th person is in the middle. Counting from the top or the bottom, the office manager is the 11th person. Thus the median salary is $75 000.

To find the middle:

- If a list has an *odd* number of values, divide by 2 and add 0.5.
  In a list of 27 numbers: $27 \div 2 + 0.5 = 14$
  → The 14th number is in the middle.
- If a list has an *even* number of values, there will be 2 numbers in the middle. Divide by 2 and use that number and the next one to find the median value.
  In a list of 38 numbers: $38 \div 2 = 19$ → The 19th and 20th numbers are in the middle.

MODE

The mode of a set of data is found by examining the data to see which value occurs most often.

Example 8

Find the mode of each of the following sets of data:

a) The number of customers per hour yesterday at Tony's Barber Shop: 6, 4, 3, 8, 4, 3, 4, 6, 4.

b) The sizes of $\frac{1}{2}$ shoes sold today at Lindon Shoes: $7\frac{1}{2}$, 6, 8, $7\frac{1}{2}$, 8, $8\frac{1}{2}$, 10, 8, 6, 7.

a) *By organizing the numbers, we can see that 4 is the mode of the data.*

3 3

4 4 4 4

6

8

b) *In this case, sizes 71/2 and 8 were equally popular so there are 2 modes. This data is called* **bimodal**.

6, 6

$7\frac{1}{2}$, $7\frac{1}{2}$, $7\frac{1}{2}$

8, 8, 8

$8\frac{1}{2}$

10

The mode of a set of data is the *value* that occurs most often. Do not confuse this with the *frequency*. If a chart shows that 10 people wear size 7 shoes, 15 people wear size 6 and 25 people wear size 8, then the mode is size 8. The frequency of this mode is 25.

THE EFFECT OF DISTRIBUTION ON MEASURES OF CENTRAL TENDENCY

If data is evenly distributed, the mean, median and mode are all very close to the middle, but data is often lopsided or *skewed*.

Consider these values that have a mean of 56.5.

34 37 45 52 55 63 81 85

The mean is not in the center. It is closer to the larger numbers at the right. The data is said to be *positively skewed*. This idea is easier to understand if we consider the three histograms below.

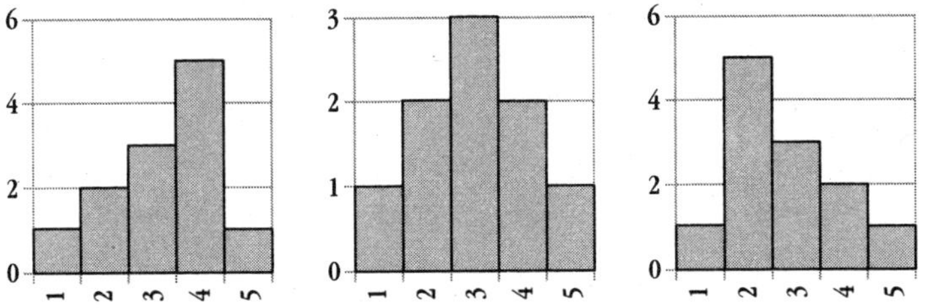

The first shows bars that trail off to the left. The data is *positively skewed.*

The middle histogram is evenly distributed. The data is not skewed.

The third shows bars that trail off to the right. The data in this case is *negatively skewed.*

The mean, median and mode will be affected by the amount that the data is skewed.

Example 9

Below is the original data for the histograms above. Find the mean, median and mode of each set of data and comment on the results.

#1. Positive skew

Value	Frequency
1	1
2	2
3	3
4	5
5	1

#2. Not skewed

Value	Frequency
1	1
2	2
3	3
4	2
5	1

#3. Negative skew

Value	Frequency
1	1
2	5
3	3
4	2
5	1

#1. Mean: $\bar{x} = \dfrac{1(1)+2(2)+3(3)+4(5)+5(1)}{12}$

$= \dfrac{39}{12} = 3.25$

Median: $\dfrac{4+3}{2} = 3.5$

Mode: 4

#2. Mean: $\bar{x} = \dfrac{1(1)+2(2)+3(3)+4(2)+5(1)}{9} = \dfrac{27}{9} = 3$

Median: 3

Mode: 3

#3. Mean: $\bar{x} = \dfrac{1(1)+2(5)+3(3)+4(2)+5(1)}{12} = \dfrac{33}{12} = 2.75$

Median: $\dfrac{3+2}{2} = 2.5$

Mode: 2

By gathering the results into a chart we can see how the distribution affects the measures of central tendency.

	Mean	Median	Mode
#1.	3.25	3.5	4
#2.	3	3	3
#3.	2.75	2.5	2

- When data is perfectly distributed, the mean, median and mode are the same and are all good estimates for the center of the data.
- When the distribution is skewed, the three measures move apart. When the distribution is skewed positively, the mean is usually lower than the median and mode. When the distribution is skewed negatively, the mean is higher.

For these reasons it is good to consider all three measures when analyzing data; however, there are some situations in which one is preferred.

- Use the mean to **predict a total**. If the mean income is $35 000 in a company employing 1200 people, multiplying 35 000 by 1200 is a good estimate of the total amount paid by the company in salaries.
- Use the median to talk about a **typical member** of the set. If the median height for a child of 5 is 110 cm, we can say that the typical 5-year-old is 110 cm. Half of all 5-year-olds are taller and half are shorter.
- Use the mode to talk about **categorical** data (such as eye color, sex, race, occupation). If there are 6 lawyers, 5 machinists, 2 farmers and 8 computer programmers, it doesn't make sense to talk about the mean or the median. In this case, there are more programmers in the group so programming is the *modal* occupation.

PRACTICE EXERCISE

1. Find the mean, median and mode, where possible, of the following sets of data:

   a) 3, 6, 8, 5, 7, 8, 3, 3, 5, 8

   b) $4.50 $2.35 $1.80 $6.45 $3.55 $4.85 $2.35

c)

Languages spoken by campers at Grandview	Frequency
French	25
English	30
Spanish	18
Greek	10

2. The following data represent the number of books read by 42 grade 6 students between September and June.

14	23	44	38	8	28	25	9	21	32	18	24	16	18
21	19	12	1	17	6	32	19	40	6	48	15	9	33
35	4	7	20	13	31	26	26	24	18	11	7	15	26

a) Determine the mean of the data.

b) What is the median number of books read?

c) Group the data into 12 intervals and prepare a frequency table of the grouped data.

d) Draw a histogram of the grouped data.

e) Which measure of central tendency best describes the distribution of the data and why?

3. Sarah has marks of 80%, 72%, 68%, 83%, 70%, 62% and 81% in 7 of her subjects. What percentage does she need in her 8th course to have an average of 75%?

4. Which measure of central tendency is appropriate in the following cases?

a) to predict the total kWh of hydro used in the province in one month

b) for a baseball cap company to decide which size to make the largest number of hats

c) to predict the income of the typical taxpayer in the province

5. In Sundown Industries there are many employees who make low wages and a few in upper management who make high salaries. If the incomes of Sundown employees are displayed in a histogram, will the distribution be negatively or positively skewed? How will the mean and median be related?

CHAPTER FOUR

Analyzing spread

The two histograms below illustrate data sets that have the same mean and median, but differ in the amount of *spread* or *variability*. It is important to investigate the degree of variability. If data is widely spread out, the measures of central tendency are less likely to accurately describe the population from which the sample was drawn.

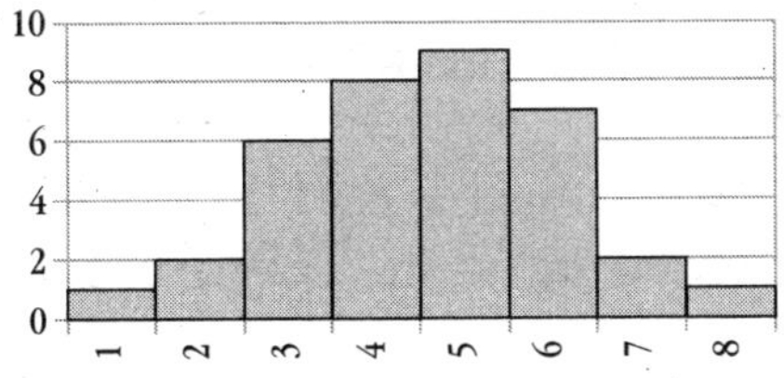

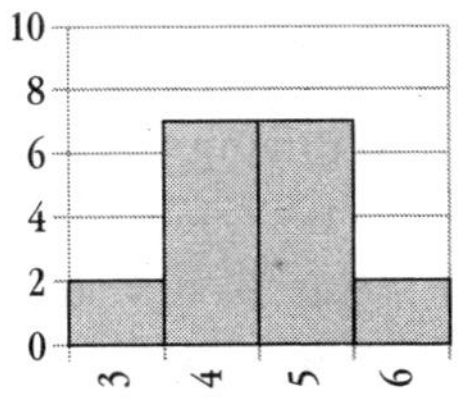

Three statistics, the *range*, the *interquartile range* and the *standard deviation* are the most commonly used methods to investigate the variability of data.

RANGE

The range is the difference between the highest and lowest values in the sample. It is valuable when we need to consider all possibilities. For example, car manufacturers take into account the wide range of driver heights by designing adjustable seats.

Example 1

The following table shows the number of Internet minutes used by the Jetson family in the last 12 months. Find the range of the data and suggest why this statistic might be important to the Jetsons.

Jan.	Feb.	Mar.	Apr.	May	Jun.	Jul.	Aug.	Sep.	Oct.	Nov.	Dec.
3500	2150	2629	2838	2107	655	864	575	1094	2103	2948	1150

The largest value is 3500 and the smallest is 575. Therefore the range is 2925. The Jetsons' usage has been between 9 and 60 hours. This knowledge could help them decide on the Internet package that is most economical for their family.

INTERQUARTILE RANGE

The range relies on only two of the values in the sample and is not a good measure of the variability of the other data. By dividing the sample into quartiles, or fourths, and ignoring the quartiles at the ends, we can investigate the spread of the central half of the data. The **interquartile range** is the region covered by the two middle quartiles.

The technique for determining the interquartile range is similar to the method for finding the median; however, there are minor differences between books which may lead to slight variations in answers. Also, if the quartiles lie between two data values, interpolation can create complications. Here we will use the following convention:

- The lower quartile, Q_L, is calculated as the $\frac{n+1}{4}$th value. If this is not an integer, **round up** to the nearest integer to approximate Q_L.
- The median, M, (which could be written Q_M) is calculated as the $\frac{n+1}{2}$th value.
- The upper quartile, Q_U, is calculated as the $3(\frac{n+1}{4})$th value. If this is not an integer, **round down** to the nearest integer to approximate Q_U.

Consider a set of 12 data values:

Since $\frac{12+1}{4} = 3.25$, round up and approximate Q_L by using the 4th piece of data.

Since $\frac{12+1}{2} = 6.5$, the median is the average of the 6th and 7th values as usual.

Since $3(\frac{12+1}{4}) = 9.75$, round down and approximate Q_U by using the 9th piece of data.

Example 2

The following data represent the monthly telephone bills (rounded to the nearest dollar) of a sample of 20 households.

56	78	120	52	39	60	86	35	55	71
63	54	30	45	57	108	74	65	79	52

Determine the interquartile range.

First, arrange the numbers in order:

30, 35, 39, 45, 52, 52, 54, 55, 56, 57, 60, 63, 65, 71, 74, 78, 79, 86, 108, 120

- *The lower quartile will be at the* $\frac{20+1}{4} = 5.25$th *position.* Q_L *can be approximated by 52, the 6th value → 25% of the data lie below 52.*
- *The upper quartile will be at the* $3(\frac{20+1}{4}) = 15.75$th *position.* Q_U *can be approximated by 74, the 15th value → 25% of the data lie above 74.*

Therefore, the interquartile range = $Q_U - Q_L = 74 - 52 = 22$.

In practice, the interquartile range is usually divided by 2 and called the semi-interquartile range. In the example above, the semi-interquartile range is 11. A statistician would say that the median of the phone bills is $58.50 and half of the bills fall within $11.00 of this amount.

BOX-AND-WHISKER PLOTS

Sometimes the interquartile range is illustrated with a **box-and-whisker plot**. The "box" surrounds the middle two quartiles and the "whiskers" extend to the ends of the data.

This is a good way to notice *outliers*. An *outlier* is a value whose distance from the box is more than 1.5 times the interquartile range.

Example 3

Display the data in example 2 in a box-and-whisker plot and identify any outliers.

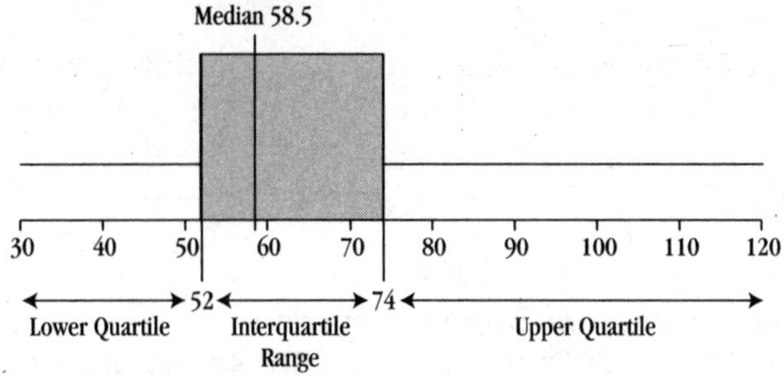

On a number line from 30 to 120, a box surrounds the data that is in the interquartile range. The lines that extend from the sides of the box to each end are called the whiskers. Since the interquartile range is 22, any value that lies more than 1.5(22) or 33 from the ends of the box is an outlier. This would include values less than 19 and greater than 107. Therefore, only 120 is an outlier.

MEAN DEVIATION

One measure of variability is the mean deviation. To "deviate" is to stray from a path. When we calculate the mean deviation we are finding the average amount that the individual values in the data have "strayed" from the mean of the distribution. The procedure is to find the distance from each value to the mean, add these answers and divide by the number of values in the sample. The formula looks like this:

Mean deviation = $\frac{\Sigma|x - \bar{x}|}{n}$, where $|x - \bar{x}|$ is the absolute value, or distance of a value x from the mean $\bar{x}$.

Example 4

The chart below shows the length of long jumps in centimetres that were done by 12 grade 8 students. Find the mean deviation of the data and explain the result.

109	120	97	143	168	102	155	124	95	126	118	117

- *Set up a table with 3 columns as shown. Under x, list the data.*
- *Calculate the mean and enter it under $\bar{x}$.*
- *Subtract column 2 from column 1; take the absolute value, and enter the answer in column 3.*

x	$\bar{x}$	$\lvert x - \bar{x} \rvert$
95	122.83	27.83
97	122.83	25.83
102	122.83	20.83
109	122.83	13.83
117	122.83	5.83
118	122.83	4.83
120	122.83	2.83
124	122.83	1.17
126	122.83	3.17
143	122.83	20.17
155	122.83	32.17
168	122.83	45.17

Example:

$$|95 - 122.83| = |-27.83| = 27.83$$

- *Add the numbers in column 3 and divide by 12 to get the mean deviation of 16.97 or 17 cm.*

$$\Sigma|x - \bar{x}| = 203.67$$

$$\frac{\Sigma|x - \bar{x}|}{12} = 16.97$$

The mean of the long jumps is 122.83 cm with a mean deviation of approximately 17 cm. This signifies that, on average, a jump is within 17 cm of the mean.

Note: It is not necessary to list the data in order in the first column; however, it illustrates the fact that the values at each end are farther from the mean than the values closer to the center.

STANDARD DEVIATION

The standard deviation is the most often used measure of variability. It is not as easy to understand as the mean variation but is important because, as we will see later, it can help us predict how far data is from the mean.

The **standard deviation** is the square root of the **variance**, which is the average of the **squares** of the deviations from the mean.

The basic formula is: $s = \sqrt{\dfrac{\Sigma(x - \bar{x})^2}{n}}$

There are several abbreviations for standard deviation. Most books use SD or *s* to denote the standard deviation for a sample and σ (pronounced sigma),which is the lowercase Greek letter for *s*, for the standard deviation of a population.

Calculators often use σ_n and σ_{n-1} for the standard deviation. See chapter 8 for details.

Example 5

Let's examine the difference between the standard deviation and the mean deviation by using data from the previous example:

The chart below shows the length of long jumps in centimetres, by 12 grade 8 students.

Ann	Pat	Lyn	Fred	Mel	Art	Ed	Tim	Flora	Orin	Ted	Sal
109	120	97	143	168	102	155	124	95	126	118	117

x	$\bar{x}$	$x - \bar{x}$	$(x - \bar{x})^2$
95	122.83	-27.83	774.51
97	122.83	-25.83	667.19
102	122.83	-20.83	433.89
109	122.83	-13.83	191.27
117	122.83	- 5.83	33.99
118	122.83	- 4.83	23.33
120	122.83	- 2.83	8.01
124	122.83	1.17	1.37
126	122.83	3.17	10.05
143	122.83	20.17	406.83
155	122.83	32.17	1034.91
168	122.83	45.17	2040.33

$$\Sigma(x - \bar{x})^2 = 5625.68$$

$$\frac{\Sigma(x - \bar{x})^2}{12} = 468.81$$

$$\sqrt{\frac{\Sigma(x\ \ \bar{x})^2}{12}} = 21.65$$

- *Set up a table with 4 columns as shown.*
- *Under x list the data.*
- *Calculate the mean and enter it under $\bar{x}$.*
- *Subtract column 2 from column 1 and enter the answers in column 3.*
- *Square the differences in column 3 and enter the results in column 4.*
- *Add the numbers in column 4 and divide by 12 to obtain the variance which is 468.81.*
- *Take the square root of the variance to find the standard deviation.*

The mean of the long jumps is 122.83 cm with a standard deviation of 21.65 cm. This is quite different from the mean deviation of 17 cm.

The first step in calculating the mean or the standard deviation is to find the difference between each value x, and the mean, $\bar{x}$.

- For values less than the mean, $x - \bar{x}$ will be negative.
- For values greater than the mean, $x - \bar{x}$ will be positive.
- Occasionally $x - \bar{x}$ may be 0.

If these differences were added, the negatives would cancel the positives. To prevent this, both formulas make all the differences positive. The mean deviation does this by taking the absolute value of the differences and the standard deviation squares the differences.

Before examining why the standard deviation is so important, let's first find an easier way to calculate it.

By squaring the binomial in the numerator and making use of the facts that:

$\frac{\Sigma x}{n} = \bar{x}$, and

$$\Sigma\bar{x} = \underbrace{\bar{x}_1 + \bar{x}_2 + \ldots + \bar{x}_n}_{n\ \text{terms}} = n\bar{x}$$

the formula for standard deviation can be reorganized to give a formula that is easier to use.

$$s = \sqrt{\frac{\Sigma(x-\bar{x})^2}{n}} = \sqrt{\frac{\Sigma(x^2 - 2x\bar{x} + \bar{x}^2)}{n}}$$

$$= \sqrt{\frac{\Sigma x^2 - \Sigma 2x\bar{x} + \Sigma\bar{x}^2}{n}}$$

$$= \sqrt{\frac{\Sigma x^2 - 2\bar{x}\Sigma x + n\bar{x}^2}{n}}$$

$$= \sqrt{\frac{\Sigma x^2}{n} - \frac{2\bar{x}\Sigma x}{n} + \bar{x}^2}$$

$$= \sqrt{\frac{\Sigma x^2}{n} - 2\bar{x}^2 + \bar{x}^2}$$

$$= \sqrt{\frac{\Sigma x^2}{n} - \bar{x}^2}$$

$$= \sqrt{\frac{(\Sigma x^2) - n\bar{x}^2}{n}}$$

The result may look similar, but the new formula $s = \sqrt{\frac{(\Sigma x^2) - n\bar{x}^2}{n}}$ does not require that the individual deviations be calculated.

Example 6

Calculate the standard deviation for example 5 using the revised formula.

List the data values under x in column 1.

Calculate the squares of these values and add to obtain

$\Sigma x^2 = 186682.$

Since $n = 12$ *and* $\bar{x} = 122.83,$

$n\bar{x}^2 = 181056.3$

Combine these results to get the standard deviation:

$$s = \sqrt{\frac{(\Sigma x^2) - n\bar{x}^2}{n}}$$

$$= \sqrt{\frac{186682 - 181056.3}{12}} = \sqrt{\frac{5625.7}{12}}$$

$$= \sqrt{468.81} = 21.65$$

x	x^2
95	9025
97	9409
102	10404
109	11881
117	13689
118	13924
120	14400
124	15376
126	15876
143	20449
155	24025
168	28224

$\Sigma x^2 = 186682$

The standard deviation is 21.65 cm.

MEASURING VARIABILITY IN GROUPED DATA

Sometimes large amounts of data have been grouped. The formula to find the standard deviation of grouped data can be found by making a small modification as follows:

$$s = \sqrt{\frac{(\Sigma x^2) - n\bar{x}^2}{n}} \rightarrow s = \sqrt{\frac{(\Sigma x^2 f(x)) - n\bar{x}^2}{n}}$$

In the new formula, x is the midpoint of an interval and $f(x)$ is the number of values in the interval.

Example 7

At Camp Wantano 6 campers have fewer than 6 mosquito bites, 3 have between 7 and 13 and one has between 14 and 20. Find the standard deviation for this data.

Since the data is grouped, we need to find the midpoint of each interval and then use the formulas for grouped data as follows:

Intervals	Midpoint	Frequency
0-6	3	6
7-13	10	3
14-20	17	1

$$\bar{x} = \frac{3(6)+10(3)+17(1)}{10} = 6.5$$

$$s = \sqrt{\frac{3^2(6)+10^2(3)+17^2(1)-10(6.5)^2}{10}} \approx 4.7$$

The standard deviation is approximately 4.7 bites. The following theorem tells us how we can interpret this statistic.

CHEBYSHEV'S THEOREM

Chebyshev's theorem uses the standard deviation to predict how far data is from the mean. The theorem states:

At least $(1 - \frac{1}{k^2})$ of data lies within k standard deviations of the mean, where $k>1$.

If k is 2, the theorem tells us that $(1 - \frac{1}{2^2})$ or $\frac{3}{4}$ of the data lies within 2 standard deviations of the mean. If k is 3, $(1 - \frac{1}{3^2})$ or $\frac{8}{9}$ of the data lies within 3 standard deviations of the mean.

Example 8

A set of data has mean 52 and standard deviation 6. Where will 75% of the data lie?

From Chebyshev's theorem we know that three-quarters or 75% of all the values will lie within 2 standard deviations of the mean. In this case, 2 standard deviations is 2(6) or 12.

Since 52 - 12 = 40 and 52 + 12 = 64, *75% of the data will lie between 40 and 64.*

Note: We can make even stronger predictions about some types of distributions. If data is distributed "normally," we can say that 95% of the data will lie within 2 standard deviations of the mean.

The ability to predict how far data is from the mean is the basis for *hypothesis* testing.
For example: An airline could assert that the monthly totals of lost bags has fallen as a result of their new luggage-handling procedures. To test this hypothesis, it is necessary to determine whether the decrease is just a chance fluctuation or if it is a direct result of the new procedures. If monthly losses were normally distributed with a mean of 20 and standard deviation of 5, we would expect that 95% of monthly losses would be between 10 and 30 bags. If losses since the initiation of new methods have been consistently lower than 7, this is **statistically significant** - that is, it is unlikely to be the result of chance and the airline's assertion is true.

PRACTICE EXERCISE

1. The following table shows the number of puppies born to a sample of 10 Jack Russell terriers:

Ember	Cassie	Spots	Nan	Bess	Daisy	Mindy	Cleo	Maggie	Brin
6	4	9	3	12	8	5	9	4	7

Find the range of the data.

2. Twenty-four grade 5 students were asked how many first cousins they had. The following data was collected:

4	5	1	3	1	6	7	2	4	1	3	5
0	3	15	2	1	4	0	4	3	8	5	3

a) Determine the interquartile range.
b) Display the data in a box and whisker plot.
c) Identify any outliers in the data.

3. Twenty dairy farmers in a community were surveyed to find out how many cows they were milking. Find the mean deviation of the results below:

21	52	105	38	40	30	42	45	78	28
35	40	43	110	56	28	86	65	32	90

4. Josee's Restaurant employs 12 waiters. On Saturday they received the following tips:

Tony	Martha	Doug	Elmer	Paul	Sanjeev
$32.75	$25.00	$58.30	$42.95	$37.50	$29.75

Dan	Jason	Cheryl	Janice	Lee	Mike
$47.00	$21.80	$63.50	$30.45	$58.25	$18.75

Calculate the standard deviation of the employees tips.

5. The table represents the weights (in kg) of 38 10-year-olds grouped in 5 kg intervals. Find the standard deviation for this grouped data.

Intervals	Frequency
23.5-28.5	4
28.5-33.5	7
33.5-38.5	9
38.5-43.5	12
43.5-48.5	5
48.5-53.5	1

6. A set of data has mean 43.5 and standard deviation 2.5. Where will 75% of the data lie?

CHAPTER FIVE

The normal distribution

THE NORMAL CURVE

The **normal probability curve** is bell-shaped and symmetric. The part of the curve to the left of the mean is identical to the part on the right. Approximately 68% of the data lie within one standard deviation of the mean and 95% lie within 2 standard deviations.

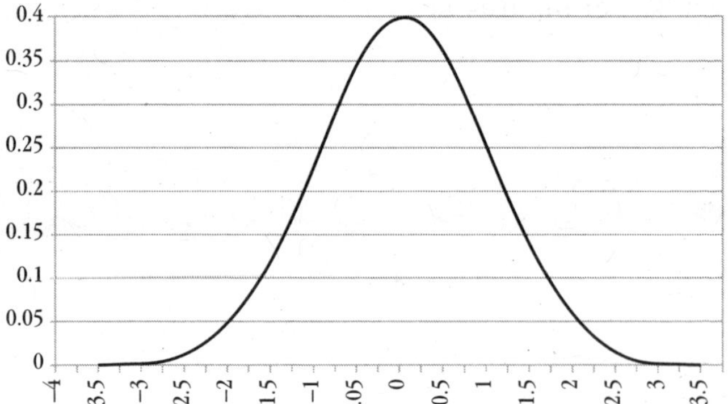

The normal curve above is described by the notation $N(0, 1)$, which signifies that it is a *normal* curve with *mean 0* and *variance 1*. (Remember that the *variance* is the square of the standard deviation).

- The total area under the curve is 1.
- The mean, median and mode are all zero.
- The curve never crosses the x axis.
- The standard deviation is 1 and is the distance from the mean to the points of inflection of the curve. These are the points

where a curve changes its concavity. A hill starts to change into a valley or a valley into a hill.

- The equation is: $y = \frac{1}{\sqrt{2\pi}} e^{x^2/2}$

A more general normal curve is described by $N\,(\mu, \sigma^2)$.

- It is bell-shaped and symmetric about the mean.
- The area under the curve is 1.
- The mean, median and mode are all μ.
- The curve never crosses the x axis.
- The standard deviation is σ.
- The equation is: $y = \frac{1}{\sigma\sqrt{2\pi}} e^{\frac{-1}{2}\left(\frac{x-\mu}{\sigma}\right)^2}$

Many real-life phenomena have frequency distributions that are approximately bell-shaped. The data clusters around the middle and the graph trails off at each end. About half the data is greater than the mean and half is less.

Example 1

Plot the frequency distribution of the data in the table that shows the lengths, rounded to the nearest centimetre, of a sample of pine boards.

Length (in cm)	150	153	156	159	162	165	168	171	174	177	180	183
Number	1	2	3	5	8	11	10	8	5	3	2	1

From the table, construct a histogram of the data.

Join the mid-points of each bar of the histogram to create the **frequency polygon** *shown here.*

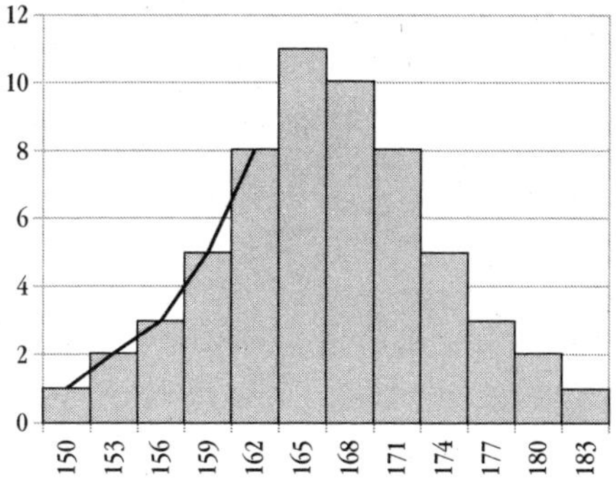

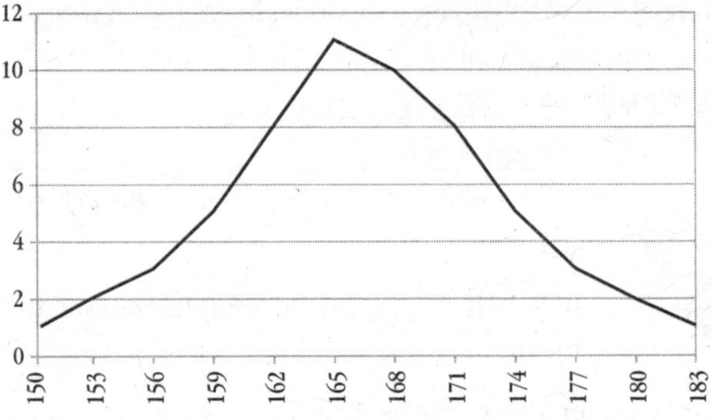

The mean is 166.5, the mode is 165 and the median is 165.

Since the standard deviation is 6.97, the variance is $(6.97)^2$ or 48.58.

Although the distribution is somewhat bell-shaped and symmetric, we can see that this is not a normal curve because the area under the curve is not equal to 1 and the mean, median and mode are not identical.

The graph of a normal distribution, with mean 166.5 and variance 48.58, looks like this:

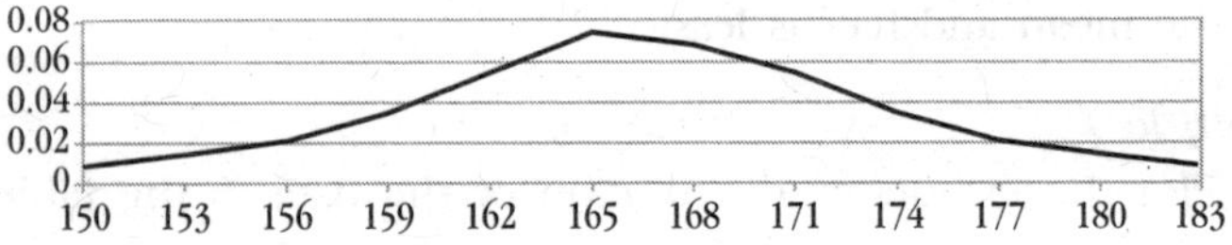

Despite the differences in the two graphs we can use this normal curve which is defined by $N(166.5, 48.58)$ to study the distribution of the lengths of the boards.

AREA PROBABILITY GRAPHS

In order to use the normal curve to study the distribution in example 1, we must first review the concept of an area probability graph. You may be familiar with this topic from your work in probability.

Example 2

Consider throwing 3 coins at once and counting the number of heads and tails. Draw the tree diagram, the frequency distribution graph and the area probability graph.

The tree diagram shows that there are 8 different possible results:

HHH, HHT, HTH, HTT,
THH, THT, TTH and TTT.

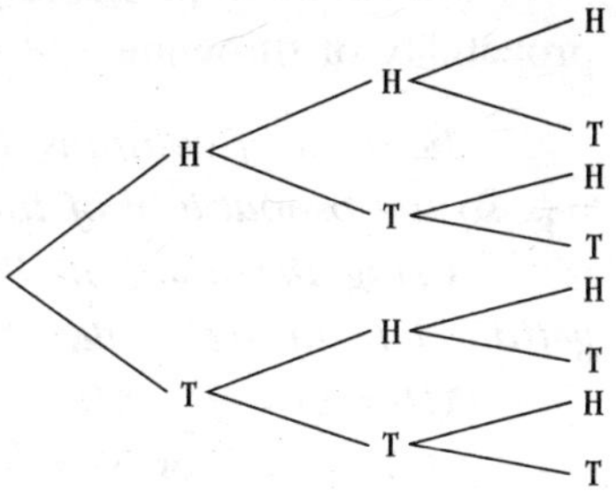

Three heads are obtained in 1 of the 8 results (HHH). Therefore the probability of getting 3 heads is $\frac{1}{8}$. Similarly, there are 3 ways to get 2 heads (HHT, HTH and THH), so the probability of getting 2 heads is $\frac{3}{8}$.

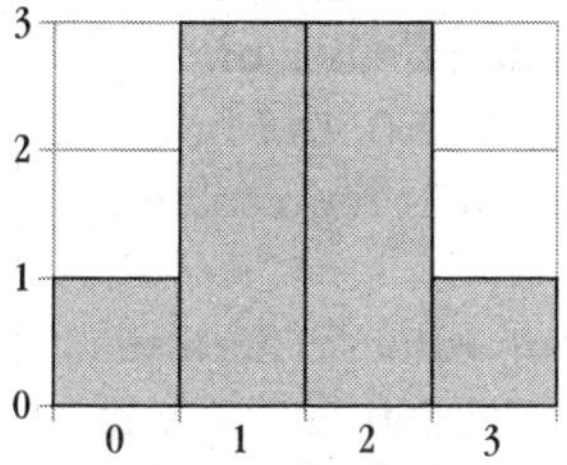

Frequency Distribution

The frequency distribution on the left shows the number of possibilities for each result.

The graph at the right shows the probability of each result. It is called an **area probability graph**, *because the area of each column is the probability of the result.*

For example, the area of the first column is $\frac{1}{8}$ which is the probability of getting 0 heads.

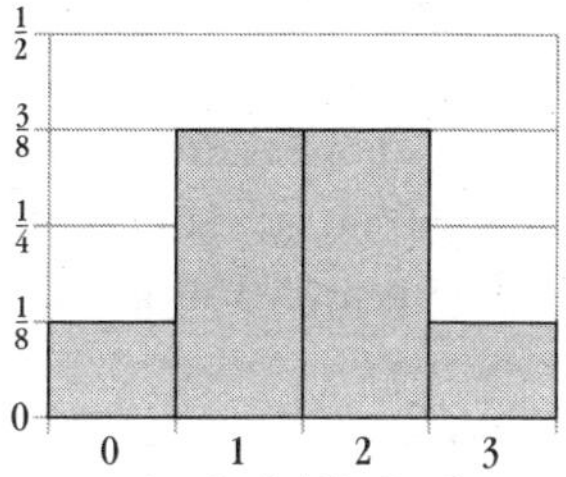

Area Probability Graph

An area probability graph can be used to find the probability of being in a particular range.

Example 3

Use the area probability graph for the coin toss to find the probability of throwing 1, 2 or 3 heads.

The area of columns 1, 2 and 3 in the graph is $\frac{1}{8}+\frac{3}{8}+\frac{3}{8}$ $=\frac{7}{8}$, *so the probability of throwing 1 to 3 heads is* $\frac{7}{8}$.

Using the notation P(H = 1) to mean the probability of getting 1 head, we could also write:

$P(H = 1) = \frac{3}{8}$. $P(H = 2) = \frac{3}{8}$ and $P(H = 3) = \frac{1}{8}$

$\therefore P(H = 1, 2, \text{or } 3) = \frac{7}{8}$.

The coin toss example deals with **discrete** values. There are only a finite number of results. The only possibilities are 0, 1, 2 or 3 and the area probability graph is represented by columns.

Many data sets deal with **continuous** values. The results can be any real numbers and the area probability graph will be a smooth curve. The probability of a result lying between 2 specific values will be the area under the curve between those 2 values.

For example, the weight of a tomato might be 254.5 g or 305.6 g. The probability of a tomato weighing between 230 g and 350 g will be the area under the probability curve between 230 and 350.

USING TABLES OF AREAS UNDER THE NORMAL CURVE

Notice that the total area in the columns of an area probability graph is 1. This is because total probability is always 1. Therefore, the normal curve is also an area probability graph. It is easy to find the area of rectangular columns but more difficult to find the area under a curve. As a result, the areas under the normal curve $N(0,1)$ for various values of X have been worked out and are available in table form.

Example 4

Find the probability that X is greater than 1.2, if X is normally distributed with mean 0 and variance 1.

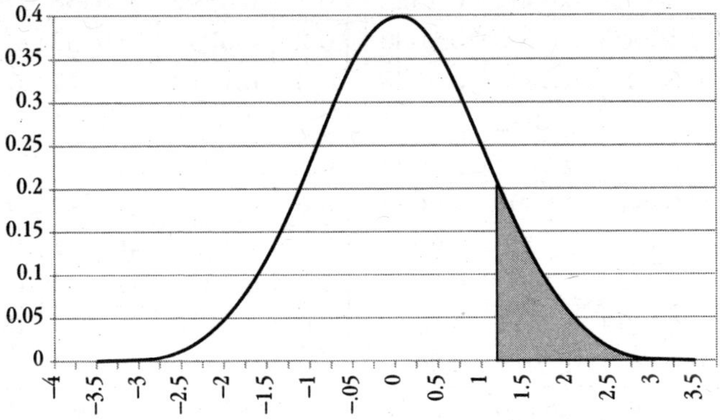

P(X > 1.2), which means the probability of a variable X being greater than 1.2 can be found by calculating the area under the normal curve N(0,1) to the right of 1.2 as shown by the shading. We can do this by using a table of areas under the normal curve.

Depending on your textbook, the table of areas under the normal curve can be printed in several ways. Here are sections of two tables. Table A gives the area under the curve to the left of the variable. Table B gives the area under the curve between the mean and the variable. Since the normal curve is symmetric, Table B only needs to give the areas for positive values.

Table A

X	0.00	0.01	0.02
-0.2	0.4207	0.4168	0.4129
-0.1	0.4602	0.4562	0.4522
0.0	0.5000	0.4960	0.5080
0.1	0.5398	0.5438	0.5478
0.2	0.5792	0.5832	0.5871
0.3	0.6719	0.6217	0.6255
0.4	0.6554	0.6591	0.6628
0.5	0.6915	0.6950	0.6985
0.6	0.7257	0.7291	0.7324
0.7	0.7580	0.7611	0.7642
0.8	0.7881	0.7910	0.7939
0.9	0.8159	0.8186	0.8212
1.0	0.8413	0.8438	0.8461
1.1	0.8643	0.8665	0.8686
1.2	0.8849	0.8869	0.8888
1.3	0.9032	0.9049	0.9066

Table B

X	0.00	0.01	0.02
0.0	0.0000	0.0040	0.0080
0.1	0.0398	0.0438	0.0478
0.2	0.0792	0.0832	0.0871
0.3	0.1719	0.1217	0.1255
0.4	0.1554	0.1591	0.1628
0.5	0.1915	0.1950	0.1985
0.6	0.2257	0.2291	0.2324
0.7	0.2580	0.2611	0.2642
0.8	0.2881	0.2910	0.2939
0.9	0.3159	0.3186	0.3212
1.0	0.3413	0.3438	0.3461
1.1	0.3643	0.3665	0.3686
1.2	0.3849	0.3869	0.3888
1.3	0.4032	0.4049	0.4066
1.4	0.4192	0.4207	0.4222

Using Table A:

The area under the curve to the left of 1.2 is 0.8849.

Therefore: $P(X < 1.2) = 0.8849$

Since the area under the entire curve is 1, the area to the right of $X = 1.2$ is 1 - 0.8849 or 0.1151.

Therefore: $P(X > 1.2) = 1 - 0.8849 = 0.1151$

Using Table B:

The area under the curve between the mean and 1.2 is 0.3849.

Therefore: $P(0 < X < 1.2) = 0.3849$

Since half the area under the curve is to the right of the mean, the area to the right of 1.2 is 0.5000 - 0.3849 or 0.1151.

Therefore: $P(X > 1.2) = P(X > 0) - P(0 < X < 1.2)$

$= 0.5000 - 0.3849 = 0.1151$

Therefore, by either method: $P(X > 1.2) = 0.1151$

Example 5

Find the probability that X is between -0.2 and 1.2, if X is normally distributed with mean 0 and variance 1.

To find $P(-0.2 < X < 1.2)$, we need to calculate the area under the normal curve $N(0,1)$ between -0.2 and 1.2 as illustrated by the shaded area:

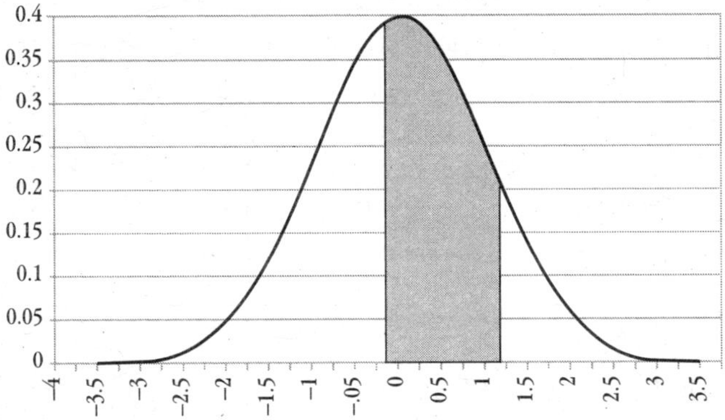

Using Table A:

$P(X < -0.2) = 0.4207$ *and* $P(X < 1.2) = 0.8849$, *so the area between them, and thus the probability can be found by subtracting:*

$P(-0.2 < X < 1.2) = 0.8849 - 0.4207 = 0.4642$

Using Table B:

$P(0 < X < 1.2) = 0.3849$

$P(0 < X < 0.2) = 0.0793$ *and since the normal curve is symmetric:*

$P(-0.2 < X < 0) = 0.0793$

The total area and thus the probability can be found by adding:

$P(-0.2 < X < 1.2) = 0.3849 + 0.0793 = 0.4642$

USING N(0,1) TO INVESTIGATE N(μ, σ²)

In order to use the area table for other normal curves, it is necessary to carry out a procedure to **standardize** the random variable X. Standardizing involves subtracting the mean from X and dividing by the standard deviation. The letter Z represents the result.

We can write:

$$Z = \frac{X - \mu}{\sigma} \text{ or } X = \sigma Z + \mu$$

What are we doing when we standardize?

Consider $N(166.5, 48.58)$, which was graphed earlier, and work out some values using the formula for Z above.

- When $X = 148$:

$$Z = \frac{148 - 166.5}{\sqrt{48.58}} = -2.65$$

- When $X = 172$:

$$Z = \frac{172 - 166.5}{\sqrt{48.58}} = 0.79$$

Although the mean of 166.5 is not in the table, if we let $X = 166.5$:

$$Z = \frac{166.5 - 166.5}{\sqrt{48.58}} = 0$$

which is the mean of $N(0,1)$.

X	Z	
148	-2.65	0.00169
150	-2.37	0.003474
152	-2.08	0.006577
154	-1.79	0.011465
156	-1.51	0.018407
158	-1.22	0.027217
160	-0.93	0.037063
162	-0.65	0.046481
164	-0.36	0.053685
166	-0.07	0.057104
168	0.22	0.055941
170	0.50	0.05047
172	0.79	0.041935
174	1.08	0.032089
176	1.36	0.022615
178	1.65	0.014678
180	1.94	0.008773
182	2.22	0.00483
184	2.51	0.002449

Graph the data, putting an X and its partner Z together on the x-axis:

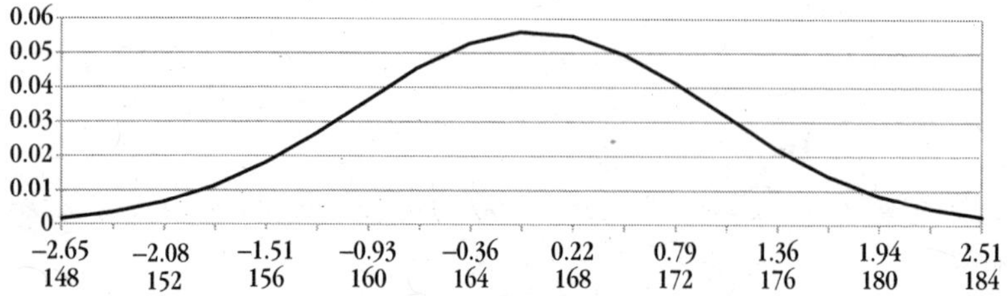

The graph shows that the probability that $X < 168$ is the same as the probability that $Z < 0.22$. Now we can use the table of areas by looking up the value of Z that corresponds to whatever value of X we are given.

Example *6*

Use the table of areas under the normal curve at the back of this book to find the probability that a random variable *X* is less than 176 if *X* is normally distributed with mean 166.5 and variance 48.58.

First standardize X: if X is 176, then: $Z = \dfrac{176 - 166.5}{\sqrt{48.58}} \approx 1.2$

Therefore: $P(X < 176) = P(Z < 1.2)$

Using the table at the back and the method for Table B:

$P(0 < Z < 1.2) = 0.3849$ *and* $P(Z < 0) = 0.5000$

Therefore: $P(Z < 1.2) = 0.3849 + 0.5000 = 0.8849$

Thus the probability that X is less than 176 is 88.49%.

It is now possible to analyze the data in example 1 using N(166.5, 48.58).

Example 7

Assume that a sample of pine boards is normally distributed with mean 166.5 cm and variance 48.58. Find the probability that a board is longer than 160 cm.

We need $P(X > 160)$.

First, standardize the variable: $Z = \dfrac{160 - 166.5}{\sqrt{48.58}} \approx -0.93$

Thus $P(X > 160)$ *is the same as* $P(Z > -0.93)$.

It is important to notice that since 160 is less than the mean in N(166.5,48.58), -0.93 is less than the mean in the distribution N(0,1). Therefore to find $P(Z > -0.93)$, *we will need to add the area below the mean and the area above the mean:*

$$P(-0.93 < Z < 0) + P(Z > 0)$$

Using the method of Table B, we know that $P(0 < Z < 0.93) = 0.3238$, *so* $P(-0.93 < Z < 0) = 0.3238$ *because of symmetry.*

Also, since 0 is the mean, $P(Z > 0) = 0.5000$.

Therefore $P(Z > -0.93) = 0.3238 + 0.5000 = 0.8238$, *and the probability that a board is longer than 160 cm is 82.38%*

It is also possible to work out the distribution when given some probabilities.

Example 8

Consider a normal distribution that has the following characteristics: $P(X > 12) = 0.0192$ and $P(X < 8) = 0.6517$. Find the mean and standard deviation.

Step 1: *Relate the probabilities to the Z values in the table.*

If $P(X > 12) = 0.0192$,

then $P(\mu < X < 12) = 0.5000 - 0.0192 = 0.4808$.

From the Table 1, $P(0 < Z < 2.07) = 0.4808$.

Thus $X = 12$ *gives the standardized value* $Z = 2.07$.

Also, $P(X < 8) = 0.6517$. *Since* 0.65 *is greater than* 0.5, *we know that 8 is to the right of the mean.*

Thus, $P(0 < X < 8) = 0.1517$.

From the table, $P(0 < Z < 0.39) = 0.1517$. *Thus* $X = 8$ *gives the standardized value* $Z = 0.39$.

Step 2: *Set up two equations using* $X = \sigma Z + \mu$ *and solve.*

$X = 12$ *and* $Z = 2.07$ $\rightarrow 12 = 2.07\sigma + \mu$

$X = 8$ *and* $Z = 0.39$ $\rightarrow 8 = 0.39\sigma + \mu$

Subtracting $\rightarrow 4 = 1.68\sigma$

$\sigma = 2.38$

Substituting back in the first equation $\rightarrow 12 = 2.07\,(2.38) + \mu$

$\mu = 7.1$

Therefore the mean is 7.1 and the standard deviation is 2.38. The notation for this distribution is N(7.1, 5.66).

Note: Remember to square the standard deviation to get the variance.

STANDARD DEVIATION AND THE NORMAL CURVE

For $N(0,1)$ the mean is 0 and the standard deviation is 1.

- $P(-1 < X < 1) + 2\,P(0 < X < 1) = 2(0.3413) = 0.6826$
  This means that approximately 68% of the data lies between -1 and 1 or that 68% of the data lies within 1 standard deviation of the mean.
- $P(-2 < X < 2) = 2\,P(0 < X < 2) = 2(0.4772) = 0.9554$
  Thus, approximately 95% of the data lies within 2 standard deviations of the mean.

By standardizing, we can show that these figures are true for all normal curves.

When data is normally distributed, approximately 68% of the data lies within 1 standard deviation of the mean and 95% of the data within 2 standard deviations.

Example 9

a) For the normal distribution $N(2,0.25)$, find the region that contains 68% of the data.

b) For $N(53, 42.25)$ find the region that contains 95% of the data.

a) *The mean is 2 and the standard deviation is 0.5. (Remember to take the square root of the variance!)*

One standard deviation below the mean is 2 - 0.5 *or* 1.5 *and one standard deviation above the mean is* 2 + 0.5 *or* 2.5.

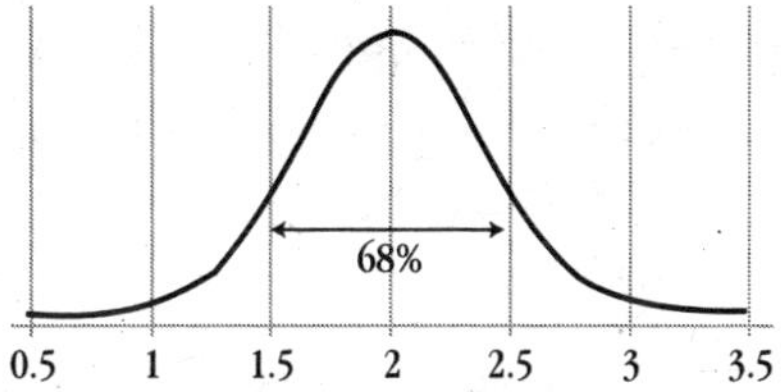

Therefore 68% of the data lies between 1.5 and 2.5.

b) *The mean is 53 and the standard deviation is 6.5.*

Two standard deviations total 2(6.5) or 13. This gives 53 - 13 *or* 40, *and* 53 + 13 *or* 66.

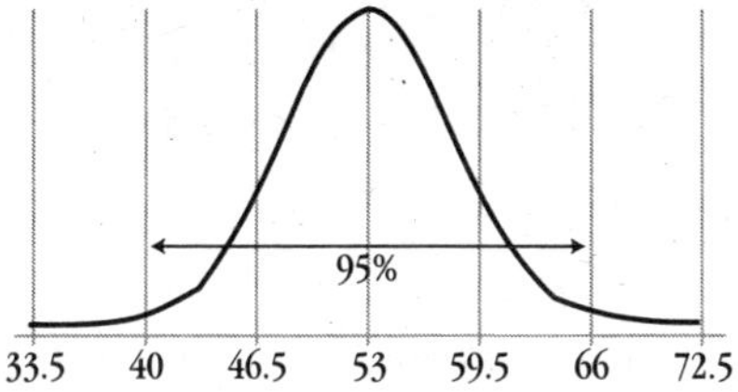

Therefore 95% of the data lies between 40 and 66.

Example 10

Consider the problem of the pine boards. The sample is normally distributed with mean 166.5 cm and variance 48.58. Between what two values do 95% of the lengths fall?

Since we are using a normal distribution to approximate the distribution of the lengths, 95% of the lengths will be within 2 standard deviations of the mean. The variance is 48.58, so one standard deviation is $\sqrt{48.58} = 6.97$ *and 2 standard deviations are 13.94. The values will be* 166.5 - 13.94 *or 152.56 and* 166.5 + 13.94 *or 180.44. Thus, 95% of the pine boards are between 152.56 cm and 180.44 cm.*

It is not always sensible to use a normal distribution to approximate the distribution of a sample of data. If the frequency polygon is very skewed the conclusions will not be valid.

PRACTICE EXERCISE

1. a) State the variance for data whose standard deviation is 4.5.
   b) Write the notation for a normal distribution whose mean is 61.7 and variance is 5.3.
   c) If data is normally distributed name three characteristics of the graph.
   d) What does $X \sim N(32, 1.6)$ signify?

2. If a random variable X is distributed normally with mean 0 and standard deviation 1, find:
   a) the probability that $X < 0.85$
   b) the probability that $X > 1.8$
   c) $P(X > -2.1)$
   d) $P(-1.2 < X < 0.64)$

3. If a random variable X has the distribution $N(30, 20.25)$, find:
   a) the probability that $X < 25$
   b) the probability that $X > 32.5$
   c) $P(X > 28)$
   d) $P(26 < X < 35)$

4. If a set of data is normally distributed with mean 35 and standard deviation 8, between what two values does 68% of the data lie?

5. If $P(X > 45) = 0.38$ and $P(X > 52) = 0.14$, find:
   a) the mean and the standard deviation
   b) $P(X < 40)$

6. A 4 L can of housepaint covers an average of 30 m^2 with a standard deviation of 2.5 m^2. Assume the coverage is normally distributed. Find the probability that Cara will have enough paint to cover her deck, which is 32 m^2, if she buys one can of paint.

7. Assume that the volume of pop placed in a bottle at a factory is normally distributed with mean 750 mL and variance 0.0001 mL. Find the probability that, on inspection, the volume of pop in a bottle will be within the permissible limits of 749.99 mL and 750.02 mL.

8. Last year the chocolate bar fundraiser at Bedford Falls School was successful, but there were too many bars unsold. The sales were approximately normally distributed. The average pupil sold 28 bars and there was a standard deviation of 9 bars. How many chocolate bars should the school order if there are 800 students and they want to sell at least 90% of the stock?

CHAPTER SIX

The normal approximation to the binomial distribution

The binomial distribution arises from experiments in which there are two possible outcomes. When the graph of such a distribution is bell-shaped, we can calculate probabilities using the table of areas under the normal curve.

THE BINOMIAL DISTRIBUTION

The prefix "bi" signifies "two," as in the word bicycle. The results of repeated experiments which are independent and identical and in which there are two possible outcomes each time is called the binomial distribution.

Example 1

Which of the following can be represented by the binomial distribution?

a) getting tails 4 times on 10 tosses of a coin

b) rolling 3 5s out of 15 rolls of a 6-sided die

c) rolling 3 5s or three 2s out of 15 rolls of a die

The first two experiments can be represented by the binomial distribution.

a) *There are 2 possible outcomes when a coin is tossed - heads and tails. Each of the 10 experiments are exactly the same and the result of 1 toss does not depend on the result of any other toss - thus they are independent and identical.*

b) *There are 6 outcomes when a 6-sided die is rolled, but in this experiment we are only interested in whether the result is a 5 or not a 5. Thus, we have an experiment with only 2 results. Each of the 15 rolls is identical and is independent of any other roll.*

c) *This experiment cannot be represented by the binomial distribution because there are 3 possible outcomes on each of the 15 trials. We could roll a 5, a 2 or another number.*

The 2 outcomes in these repeated (or Bernoulli) trials are usually referred to as success and failure. It is not necessary for them to be equally possible.

Example 2

Calculate the probabilities for success and failure on each trial in the following situations:

a) getting tails 4 times on 10 tosses of a coin

b) rolling 3 5s out of 15 rolls of a 6-sided die

a) *The two possible outcomes in each of the 10 trials are heads and tails. We can consider throwing a tail as a success. Then the probability of success on each trial is* $p = \frac{1}{2}$ *and the probability of failure (i.e., getting a head) is* $q = 1 - p = 1 - \frac{1}{2} = \frac{1}{2}$.

b) *We can think of rolling a 5 as a success and not rolling a 5 as a failure. This situation is different from the coin tossing experiment because the probabilities are not equal. The probability of success on each of the 15 trials is* $p = \frac{1}{6}$, *while the probability of failure on each trial is* $q = 1 - p = 1 - \frac{1}{6} = \frac{5}{6}$.

So far we have only worked out the probabilities for success or failure on one trial but we can use these to find the probability of a specific number of successes in a number of trials.

Example 3

Consider tossing a coin 3 times.

a) Calculate the probability distribution for these repeated trials.

b) Graph the probability distribution and comment on its shape.

a) *If we tossed a coin 3 times we might get 3 heads or 3 tails or a combination of heads and tails. The possibilities can be displayed in a tree diagram:*

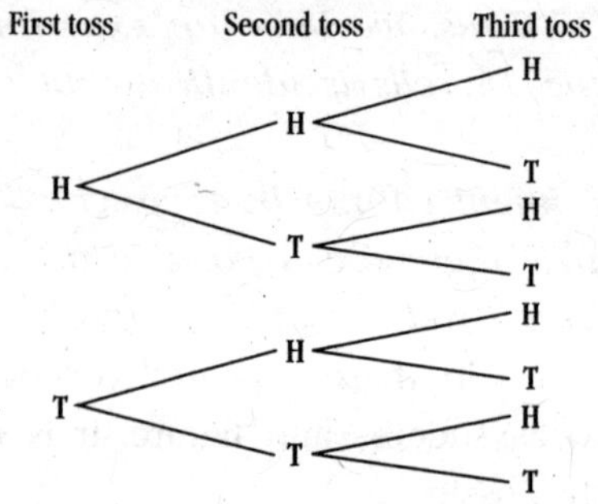

There are a total of 8 possible outcomes. If H is considered to be a success, then HHH represents 3 successes and the probability of 3 successes is $p(3) = \frac{1}{8}$.

Similarly, $p(2) = \frac{3}{8}$, $p(1) = \frac{3}{8}$ *and* $p(0) = \frac{1}{8}$.

Instead of using a tree diagram we can work out these probabilities by using the formula for the binomial distribution:

$p(x) = \binom{n}{x} p^x q^{n-x}$ gives:

$$p(3) = \binom{3}{3}\left(\frac{1}{2}\right)^3\left(\frac{1}{2}\right)^{3-3} = \binom{3}{3}\left(\frac{1}{2}\right)^3\left(\frac{1}{2}\right)^0 = 1\left(\frac{1}{8}\right)(1) = \frac{1}{8}$$

$$p(2) = \binom{3}{2}\left(\frac{1}{2}\right)^2\left(\frac{1}{2}\right)^{3-2} = \binom{3}{2}\left(\frac{1}{2}\right)^2\left(\frac{1}{2}\right)^1 = 3\left(\frac{1}{4}\right)\left(\frac{1}{2}\right) = \frac{3}{8}$$

$$p(1) = \binom{3}{1}\left(\frac{1}{2}\right)^1\left(\frac{1}{2}\right)^{3-1} = \binom{3}{1}\left(\frac{1}{2}\right)^1\left(\frac{1}{2}\right)^2 = 3\left(\frac{1}{2}\right)\left(\frac{1}{4}\right) = \frac{3}{8}$$

$$p(0) = \binom{3}{0}\left(\frac{1}{2}\right)^0\left(\frac{1}{2}\right)^{3-0} = \binom{3}{0}\left(\frac{1}{2}\right)^0\left(\frac{1}{2}\right)^3 = 1(1)\left(\frac{1}{8}\right) = \frac{1}{8}$$

For those who haven't studied probability, the following is a brief explanation of the terms in the formula $p(x) = \binom{n}{x} p^x q^{n-x}$:

• $p(x)$ means the probability of x successes. Thus $p(1)$ is the probability of 1 success.

• $\binom{n}{x}$ is the number of ways of getting x successes in n trials.

Thus $\binom{3}{2}$ is the number of ways of getting 2 successes in 3 trials.

Since we can get SSF, SFS or FSS, $\binom{3}{2}$ is 3.

Rather than list all possibilities, $\binom{n}{x}$ can be evaluated using the following formula:

$$\binom{n}{x} = \frac{n!}{x!(n-x)!}, \text{ e.g., } \binom{3}{2} = \frac{3!}{2!\,1!} = \frac{6}{2(1)} = 3 \text{ and } \binom{5}{2} = \frac{5!}{2!\,3!} = \frac{120}{2(6)} = 10.$$

Note: The exclamation mark denotes factorial notation. 4! means $4 \times 3 \times 2 \times 1$. Most calculators have a factorial notation button which makes evaluation easier.

$$\text{If } p \text{ is } \frac{2}{3}, \text{ then } p^3 = \left(\frac{2}{3}\right)^3 = \frac{8}{27}.$$

• p^x denotes the probability of x successes.

• q^{n-x} denotes the probability of $n - x$ failures. Since there are only two outcomes, if there are x successes, there will be $n - x$ failures.

$$\text{If } p \text{ is } \frac{2}{3}, \text{ then } q \text{ is } \frac{1}{3}, \text{ and } q^{5-3} = \left(\frac{1}{3}\right)^2 = \frac{1}{9}.$$

b) *The graph of the distribution is just the area probability graph. It shows the probabilities for each result.*

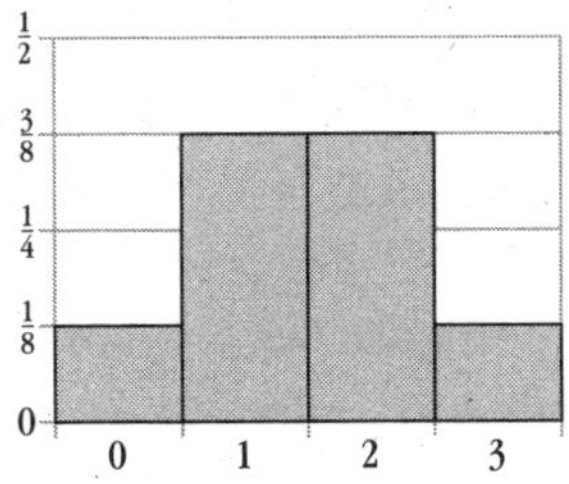

COMPARING THE BINOMIAL DISTRIBUTION TO THE NORMAL DISTRIBUTION

In the coin-tossing experiment, the binomial distribution produced a graph similar to one for a normal distribution. It is approximately bell-shaped and symmetric about the mean. However, the binomial distribution can produce a variety of graphs. The shape will depend on the values of n and p.

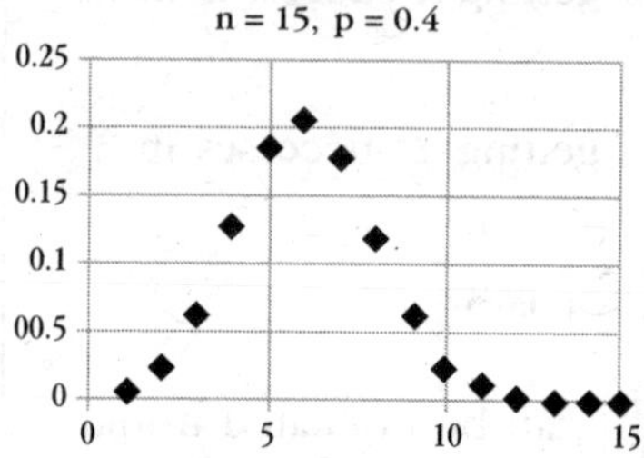

Here is the graph of a binomial distribution with 15 trials where the probability of success is 0.4.

It has a shape quite similar to the normal curve.

The two graphs below show binomial distributions, also with 15 trials. The first has probability of success 0.25 and the second has probability of success 0.75.

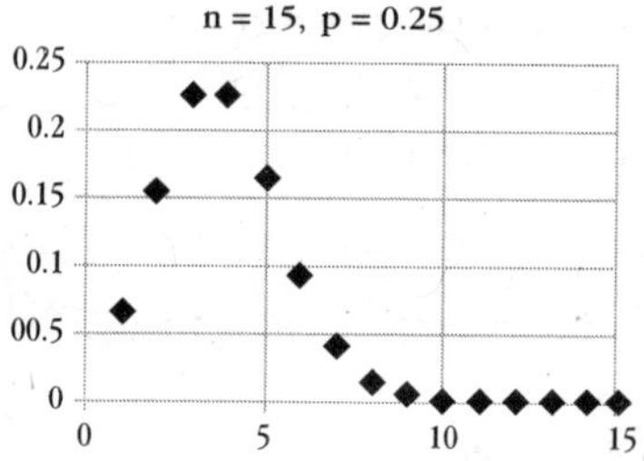

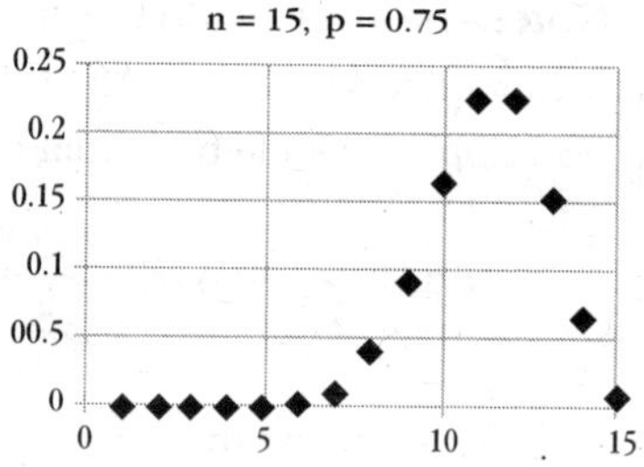

Notice that these two graphs are very skewed. They do not resemble the normal curve.

USING THE NORMAL DISTRIBUTION TO APPROXIMATE THE BINOMIAL DISTRIBUTION

An example can demonstrate why it is advantageous to use the normal distribution to approximate a binomial distribution if possible.

Example 4

If the probability of a raft tipping over when navigating a particular set of rapids is 0.25, what is the probability that fewer than 61 rafts out of 200 will tip over when traversing the rapids?

To calculate the probability, we need to find :

$P(X \leq 60) = p(0) + p(1) + p(2) + \ldots + p(60)$, *which represents the probability that no rafts will tip, plus the probability that 1 will tip, plus the probability that 2 will tip, and so on, up to the probability that 60 will tip.*

Since calculating p(60) alone requires us to work out $\binom{200}{60}(0.25)^{60}(0.75)^{14}$ *it is obvious that it would be much easier to use the normal distribution tables to approximate the answer if we could.*

> In order to use the normal tables to analyze a binomial distribution, we need to calculate a mean μ, and a variance σ^2. The formulas $\mu = np$ and $\sigma^2 = npq$ are considered to be good approximations as long as np and nq are both larger than 5.

Example 5

Find approximations for the mean and variance for the following binomial distributions if appropriate.

a) A distribution with $n = 15$ and p = 0.25

b) A distribution with $n = 20$ and p = 0.45

a) *First calculate np and nq:*

$np = 15(0.25) = 3.75$

and $nq = 15(1\text{-}0.25) = 15(0.75) = 11.25$

Since np is less than 5, this binomial distribution cannot be approximated by a normal distribution.

b) *Calculate np and nq:*

$np = 20(0.45) = 9$ *and* $nq = 20(1\text{-}0.45) = 20(0.55) = 11$

Since they are both larger than 5, we can calculate an approximate mean and variance:

$\mu = np = 20(0.45) = 9$ *and* $\sigma^2 = npq = 9(0.55) = 4.95$

Thus the distribution can be approximated by N (9,4.95).

It is now possible to investigate the rafting question without calculating 61 different probabilities.

Example 6

If the probability of a raft tipping over when navigating a particular set of rapids is 0.25, what is the probability that fewer than 61 rafts out of 200 will tip over when traversing the rapids?

First calculate np and nq:

$np = 200(0.25) = 50$ *and* $nq = 200(1 - 0.25) = 200(0.75) = 150$

Since np and nq are both larger than 5, we can calculate an approximate mean and variance:

$\mu = np = 200(0.25) = 50$ *and* $\sigma^2 = npq = 50(0.75) = 37.5$

Therefore the distribution can be approximated by N (50,37.5).

The binomial distribution deals with discrete data while the normal distribution is continuous. We compensate for this difference by extending the values 0.5 units to each side. For example, 10 in the binomial distribution would range from 9.5 to 10.5 in the normal distribution. Thus $P(X \leq 10)$ in the binomial distribution is approximated by $P(X \leq 10.5)$ in the normal distribution and $P(X = 10)$ by $P(9.5 \leq X \leq 10.5)$

$P(X \leq 60)$ *is approximated to* $P(X \leq 60.5)$ *in the normal distribution.*

Standardizing gives: $Z = \dfrac{60.5 - 50}{\sqrt{37.5}} = 1.714$

$P(X \leq 60.5) = P(Z \leq 1.714) = 0.9564$

Therefore, there is approximately a 95.6% probability that fewer than 61 rafts out of 200 will tip over.

PRACTICE EXERCISE

1. Which of the following can be represented by the binomial distribution?
   a) Martin scoring 6 times out of 20 free throws in basketball
   b) drawing a king or an ace 4 times out of 15 draws from a standard deck of 52 cards
   c) rolling 4 2s out of 12 rolls of a 6-sided die

2. Calculate the probabilities for success and failure in the following situations:
   a) getting an even number with a 6-sided die
   b) choosing a king from a standard deck of 52 cards
   c) being born on a Sunday

3. Brian has a 1 in 4 chance of hitting a homerun each time he comes to bat. Consider his performance in 4 times at bat:
   a) Calculate the probability distribution for these repeated trials.
   b) Graph the probability distribution and comment on its shape.

4. Decide if each of the following binomial distributions can be approximated by a normal distribution. Find approximations for the mean and variance if appropriate.
   a) a distribution with $n = 84$ and $p = 0.65$
   b) a distribution with $n = 8$ and $p = 0.35$

5. In a factory that produces car parts, an average of 3% of door handles are defective. What is the probability that fewer than 4 handles are defective out of an order of 200?

6 A die is thrown 30 times. If a success is defined as rolling a 3 or a 5, determine the probability of getting exactly 15 successes in the 30 trials by using the normal approximation to the binomial distribution.

7. If the probability of catching the flu this winter is 0.40, what is the probability that more than half of the 50 staff at Highcrest School will catch the flu?

CHAPTER SEVEN

Two variable statistics

Consider these commonplace assertions based on statistics:

- Smoking is a leading cause of lung cancer.
- Fluoride prevents cavities.
- Seat belts save lives.

Although our study thus far has been focused on single variable statistics, many familiar statements deal with the relationship between two things.

Two variable statistics are the basis for many decisions in business and government. When research showed a strong correlation between smoking and lung cancer, antismoking laws became the norm. Seat belts were mandated when data proved conclusively that their use was statistically related to saved lives in motor-vehicle accidents. Fluoride was added to drinking water in many places when its presence was linked to lower levels of tooth decay.

Although most two-variable statistical tests are beyond the scope of high-school work, this chapter will examine a few basic techniques which are covered in greater detail in university courses.

SCATTERPLOTS

Scatterplots are graphs consisting of ordered pairs representing the two sets of data that are being compared.

Example 1

Ace Tutoring wants to put out an advertising brochure to show that students who spend more time at Ace achieve higher math marks. They collected the following data for 20 students who were failing math.

Hours	Mark	Hours	Mark	Hours	Mark	Hours	Mark
5	65	12	74	7	62	20	93
7	72	10	74	13	83	18	82
3	56	8	75	10	80	15	85
12	80	5	58	3	61	8	70
9	75	1	51	7	67	6	65

Display the data in a scatterplot and comment on the graph.

First, use the horizontal axis to represent the hours of tutoring and the vertical axis to represent the final math mark.

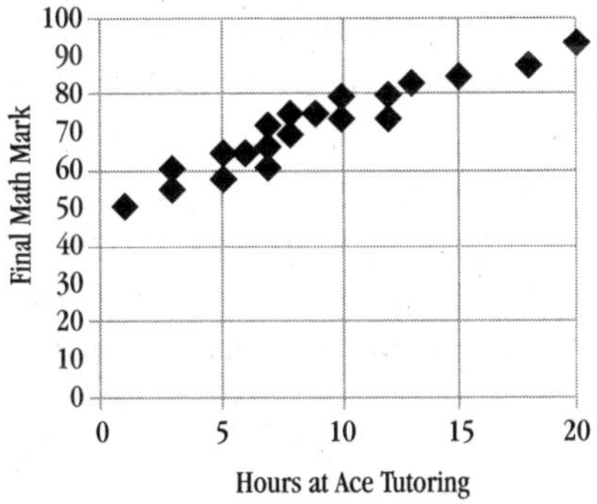

Plot ordered pairs in which the first number gives the hours of tutoring and the second, the final math mark.

The points in the scatterplot show a small but definite trend up and to the right. We say that the variables are **positively correlated** *because the group clusters about a line that has a positive slope.*

This is good news for the tutoring company because it appears that students who study with them do better in math; however, a skeptical person might point out that a student who studied math for 20 hours *at home* might also get 93%. In other words, there may not be a **causal relationship** between the two variables.

Example 2

A camp outfitter offers 12 different sleeping bags. Data on the temperature rating and cost of the bags is as follows:

Temp.(°C)	Cost($)	Temp. (°C)	Cost($)	Temp.(°C)	Cost($)
to 15°	21.99	to -30°	185.99	to 0°	59.99
to -10°	79.99	to 8°	39.99	to -10°	99.99
to 0°	49.99	to 0°	54.99	to 8°	26.99
to -30°	156.99	to -35°	201.99	to -10°	109.99

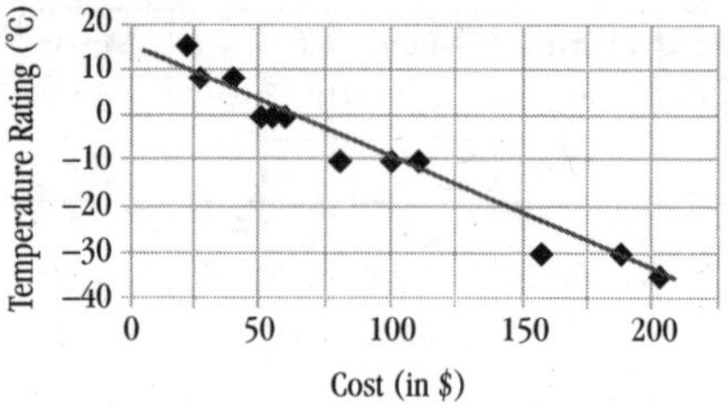

Display the data in a scatterplot and discuss any noticeable pattern.

The horizontal axis represents the cost of the sleeping bags and the vertical represents the lowest temperature rating in °C.

The points show a trend downwards and to the right. They cluster around a line with a negative slope.

Therefore, we would say that there is a **negative correlation** *between the cost of the bags and the temperature rating. As a sleeping bag gets more expensive, the temperature rating goes down.*

This is not surprising, since a bag to resist colder temperatures probably needs more fill, or a more costly type of fill. Thus there is a causal relationship between the two variables: an increased quality or quantity of fill causes an increase in the price.

Example 3

Plot the following set of data that gives the shoe sizes of 15, 14-year-old girls and the number of sit-ups they can perform in 30 seconds.

Shoe Size	Sit-ups	Shoe Size	Sit-ups	Shoe Size	Sit-ups
8	10	5	28	8	12
7	25	6	20	8	14
7	14	6	13	7	17
6	16	5	15	6	15
7	22	7	7	4	14

Display this data in a scatterplot and comment on its shape.

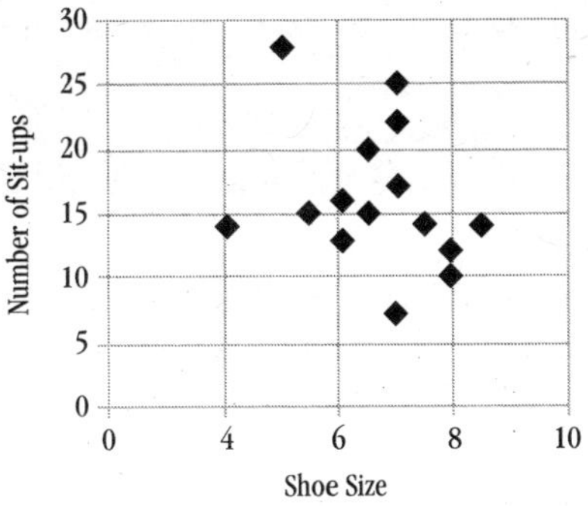

The scatterplot shows neither a positive nor a negative correlation. The points are distributed randomly. For example, some girls with size 7 shoes can do many sit-ups and some can hardly do any.

This is not surprising. We would not expect that shoe size and the number of sit-ups a 14-year-old girl can do would be related.

However, the relationship between two variables must be analyzed carefully. A scatterplot of the shoe sizes of 100 grade-school children and the number of sit-ups they could perform might show a strong positive correlation. Why? Consider the fact that grade 1 children probably have smaller feet than grade 8s and can do fewer sit-ups!

It is possible for data to show a positive or negative correlation even though changing the value of one variable will not affect the value of the other. That is, variables can be correlated even if there is no causal relationship between the two.

LINE OF BEST FIT

If the scatterplot shows a strong positive or negative correlation (and there is a causal relationship between the two variables), we would like to use the graph to predict other values.

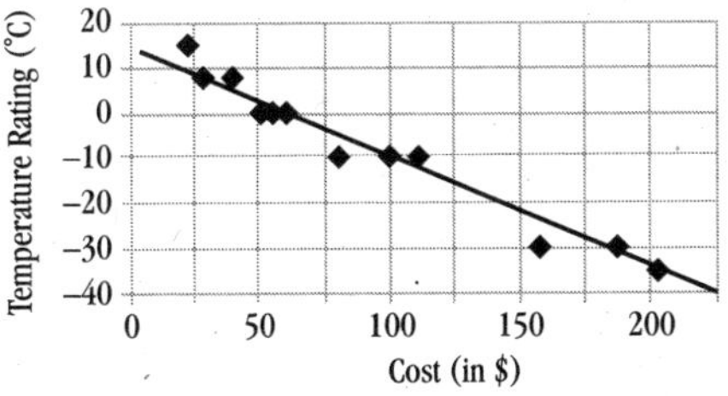

For example, from the sleeping bag scatterplot we might conclude that a bag to withstand temperatures of -40°C will cost around $225.00.

Our prediction is based on a line drawn through the cluster of points called a **line of best fit**.

One way to construct a line of best fit is to draw a line through the points so that:

- as many points as possible lie on the line
- approximately half the points lie above the line and half lie below the line

This is called an eyeball-fit line. Using any two points on the line we can write an equation.

If a scatterplot has an outlier, a point that is far away from the cluster, it should be ignored when drawing an eyeball-fit line.

Example 4

Draw an eyeball-fit line through the following scatterplot and write an equation.

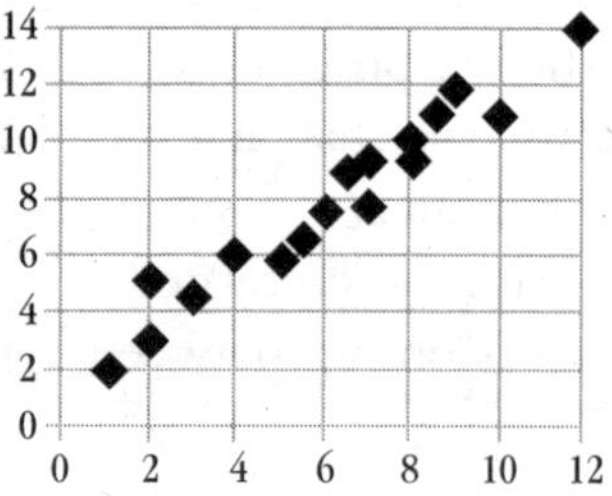

Seven points lie above the line and seven below. The line passes through 3 data points.

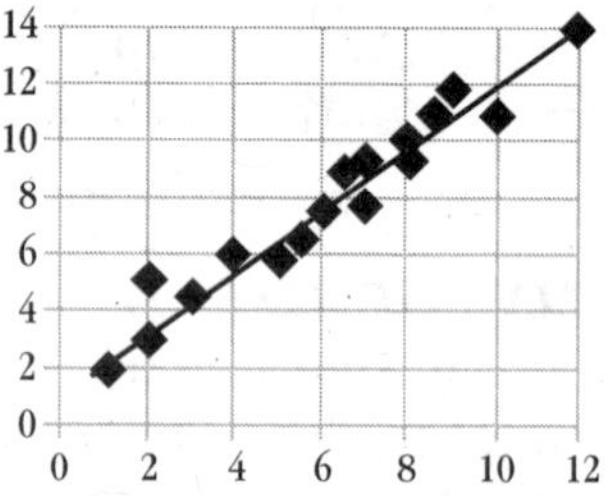

Two of the points on the line are (1,2) and (12,14). Using these points we can calculate the slope m, and write an equation for the line.

$$m = \frac{14-2}{12-1} = \frac{2}{11} \qquad y - y_1 = m\,(x - x_1)$$

$$\therefore y - 2 = \frac{12}{11}(x - 1)$$

$$\therefore 11y - 22 = 12x - 12$$

$$\therefore 12x - 11y + 10 = 0$$

The line $12x - 11y + 10 = 0$ *is only a summary of the data in the scatterplot. Some data points lie above the line and some below the line.*

Sometimes it is hard to be sure that the line drawn is really the best choice. One method that avoids guessing is based on the idea that if we calculate the squares of the vertical distances from the data points to a particular line and add them up, the sum should be as small as possible. The line is called the *least squares line* or the *regression line*. A graphics calculator produces a line of best fit using this method. See chapter 8 for more details.

CURVE OF BEST FIT

In many cases a curve may summarize data better.

Example 5

Consider the following scatterplots. Sketch a curve that seems to fit the data and identify its type.

a)

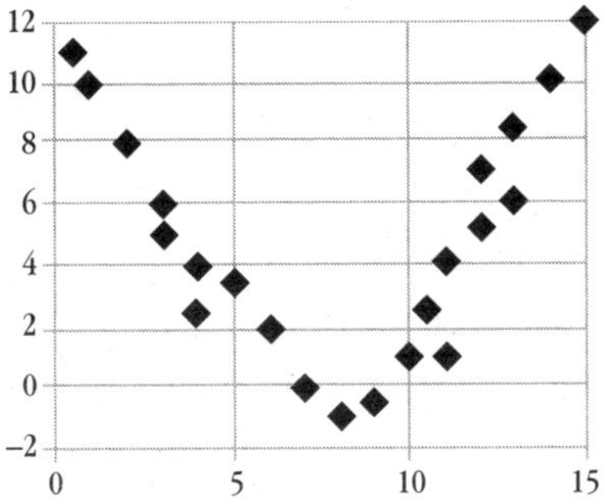

b)

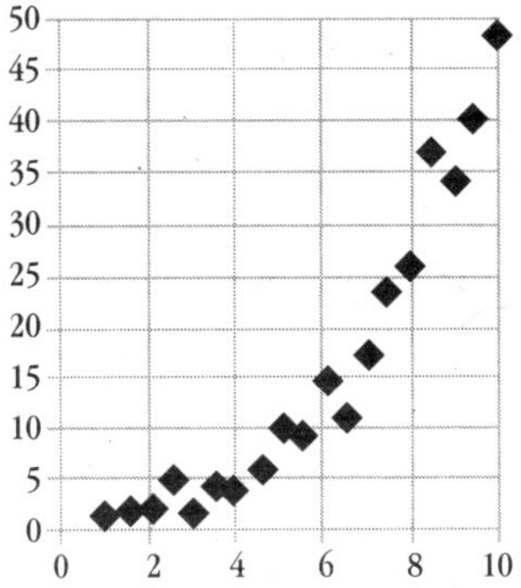

a) *A parabolic curve shows the general trend of this data. Therefore a quadratic function could be developed to approximate the data.*

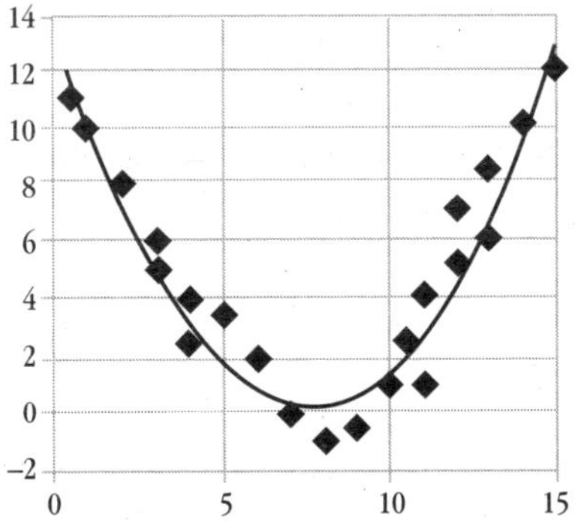

b) *A curve drawn through this data sweeps up and to the right like a growth curve. An exponential function would describe this data.*

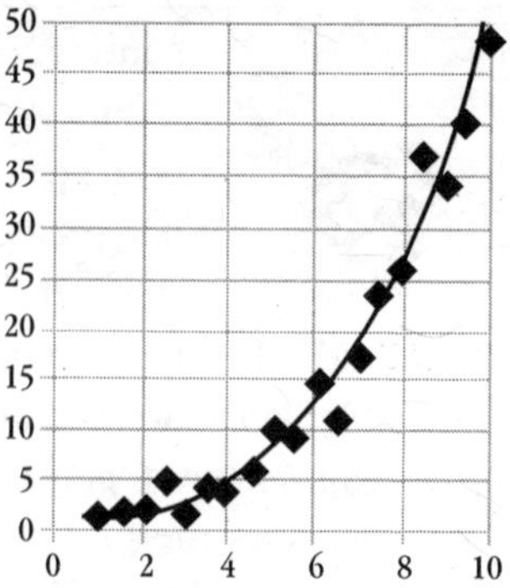

Although we can sometimes identify the type of curve required, it is often difficult to formulate the equation. Some calculators and spreadsheets will fit a curve and display the equation. See chapter 8 for more details.

CORRELATION

From the scatterplot we can see if there is a positive or negative correlation by examining the line or curve of best fit. If one variable increases as the other increases, the correlation is positive. If one variable decreases as the other increases, the correlation is negative.

We sometimes also identify the relationship as *strong* or *weak*. Data that tightly hugs the line or curve of best fit shows a strong correlation. Data that clusters loosely around the line or curve displays a weak correlation.

Example 6

Identify whether the following scatterplots have:

- a strong or weak positive correlation
- a strong or weak negative correlation
- no correlation

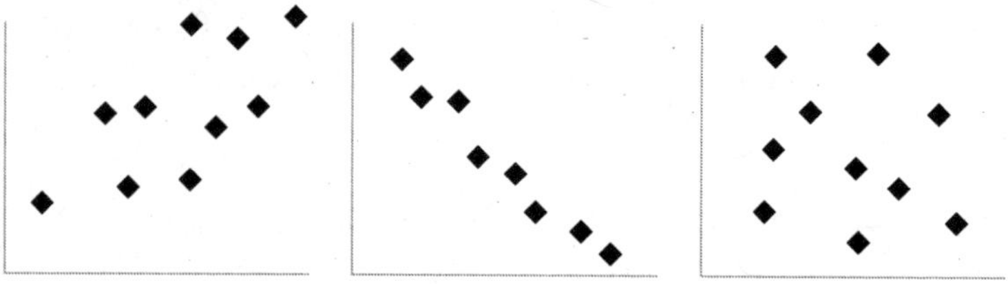

The first graph shows a weak positive correlation. Points are loosely clustered around an imaginary line with a positive slope. The second plot shows a strong negative correlation. If we drew a line through these points, many would be on the line or very close to it. The third scatterplot shows points in a random pattern. There is no correlation.

PRACTICE EXERCISE

1. George's Appliances carries 12 models of refrigerators. The table shows the total capacity and the predicted yearly electricity requirement (in kWh).

Total Cu. Ft. Cap.	kWh/year	Total Cu. Ft. Cap.	kWh/year	Total Cu. Ft. Cap.	kWh/year
18.1	583	21.6	714	16.8	567
20.1	583	2.4	283	4.3	321
9.5	540	15.2	560	25.2	825
17.4	438	12.1	540	21.1	777

Display the data in a scatterplot and discuss any noticeable pattern.

2. The scatterplot shown compares yearly family income and graduation averages for a group of 18 students. Comment on the relationship of the variables with respect to correlation and causation.

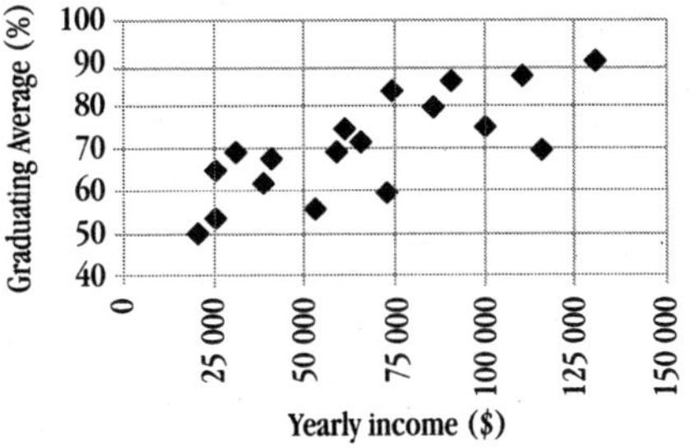

3. Draw an eyeball-fit line for the scatterplot and using two points find an equation for the line.

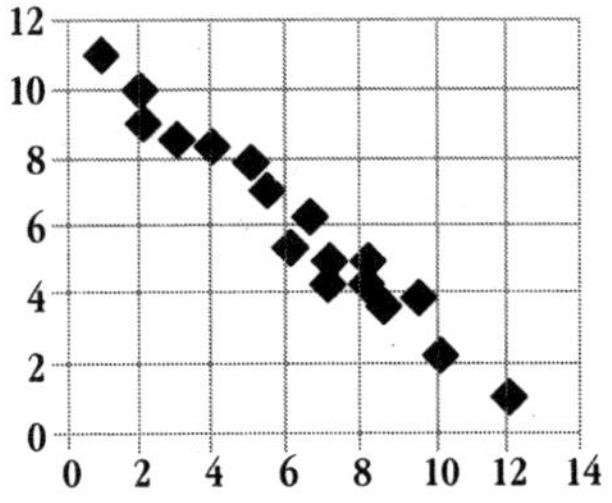

4. Sketch and identify a possible curve of best fit for the scatterplot given.

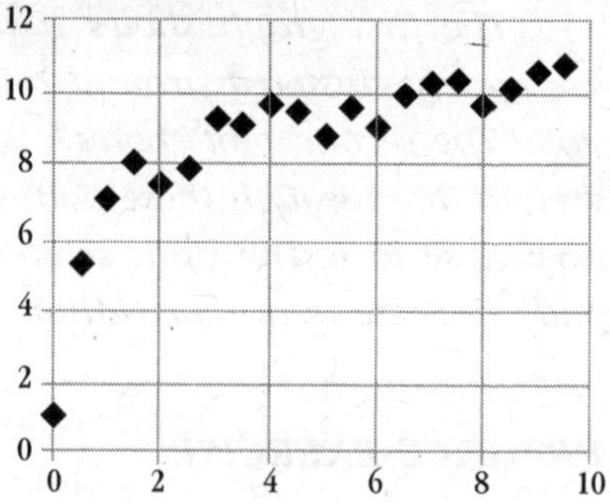

5. Identify whether the following scatterplots have:
   - a strong or weak positive correlation
   - a strong or weak negative correlation
   - no correlation

a)

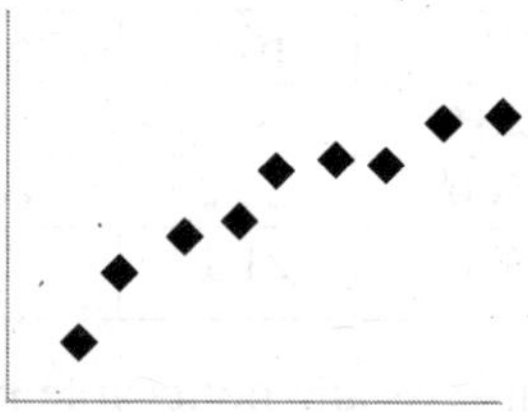

b)

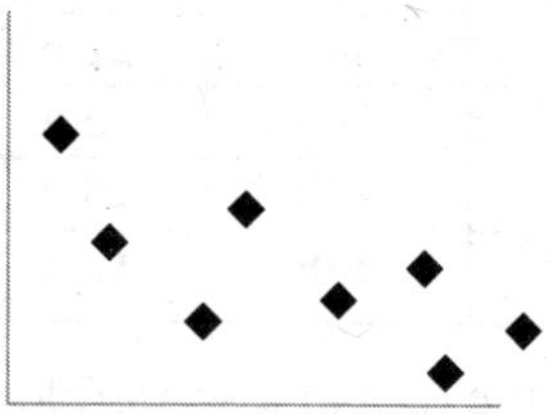

CHAPTER EIGHT

Using calculators and computers in statistics

Statistical calculations can often be tedious and it is easy to make errors when dealing with large sets of data. For these reasons, technology offers great advantages to the statistics student. There are statistics programs such as Minitab which can construct graphical and numerical summaries and perform complicated statistical tests. However, students can carry out most of the procedures required at the high-school level using a scientific calculator and a simple spreadsheet such as MSWorks or early versions of Clarisworks, which are available in many schools. More powerful spreadsheets such as Microsoft Excel and Quattro Pro have basic statistical features built in and some also have a data-analysis package that can be loaded.

It is worth the effort to become familiar with the features of your calculator and a computer spreadsheet. With less need to worry about calculations you can concentrate on the really important part of statistics - analysis of the data.

CONDUCTING SIMULATIONS

Simulations are frequently carried out with computer programs such as spreadsheets.

Example 1

Robin wants to simulate guessing the answers on a 10-question test. Each question has 3 answers but only 1 is correct. He wants to estimate the probability of getting exactly 6 correct. How can he do this using a spreadsheet?

There are 3 possible answers to each question so Robin needs to choose a method which gives a probability of $\frac{1}{3}$. *He enters a command in cell A2 to produce number 1, 2 or 3. If Robin copies this command down to cell A11 he will have a simulation of guessing the answers on the test. He can repeat the experiment as often as he wants, to work out the probability of getting exactly 6 correct answers.*

In Microsoft Works

	A	B	C
1	Answer		
2	=Int(Rand()*3)+1		

In Clarisworks

	A	B	C
1	Answer		
2	=Rand(3)		

Int(Rand()*3)+1

This command in Microsoft Works produces the numbers 1, 2 and 3 in the following way.

Rand() gives a random number between 0.000 and 0.999.

*3 multiplies this number by 3, producing a number between 0.000 and 2.997

Int causes the program to take only the integer part of the number, 0, 1 or 2

+1 adds 1 to the result above to produce 1, 2 or 3

Example 2

(See chapter 1, example 6 for an alternate solution)

The student council is running a school carwash to raise money. The students hope to attract 30 cars in 6 hours. Three students can wash one car in 10 minutes. Geoff, the council president, wants to work out how many students to schedule to avoid lineups. How can he use a simulation to help?

Geoff needs to model this problem using a probability of 1 in 12. He enters the command to generate the numbers 1 to 12 in A2 and chooses 7 to represent a car arriving. He then copies the command down to A361 to simulate the entire 6-hour carwash.

In Microsoft Works

	A	B	C	D
1	Int(Rand()*12)+1			
2				

Once the simulation is finished, Geoff can count how frequently the number 7 appears within any 10 lines in column A. This lets him estimate how often cars will arrive closer than 10 minutes apart. He can also estimate waiting times and thus make a decision about how many carwash teams to run.

SORTING AND ORGANIZING DATA

On a calculator

Inexpensive scientific calculators do not sort data but graphics calculators do. In the TI-81, for example, if data is entered as follows:

x_1	5
y_1	1
x_2	3
y_2	1
x_3	2
y_3	1
x_4	5
y_4	1

and then the x-sort function is used, the data will rearrange as shown at the right.

x_1	2
y_1	1
x_2	3
y_2	1
x_3	5
y_3	1
x_4	5
y_4	1

With a spreadsheet

All spreadsheets will sort data in ascending or descending order. This feature makes it much easier to find the median and the mode.

DISPLAYING DATA

On a calculator

Although graphics calculators do not draw bar, line and circle graphs from entered data, they can produce histograms and scatterplots.

With a spreadsheet

Spreadsheets do a wonderful job of displaying data. Most offer a wide range of graphing options from bar and line graphs to separated pie graphs. Labels on axes, titles and legends can all be added and edited. Once data is entered in the spreadsheet columns and selected, the program leads you through the steps to create displays that can be printed, or copied, to other programs such as WordPerfect or Microsoft Word.

If you can't find **histogram** in your spreadsheet program, choose a column graph and find the option that allows you to format the column width. The gap between the bars on the graph can be eliminated to produce a histogram.

FINDING THE MEAN, MEDIAN, MODE AND QUARTILES

On a calculator

If your calculator has the symbols $\bar{x}$ and Σ+, or the words STAT or DATA, you can use it to find the mean. Look at the instruction book (if you kept it!) or try the following experiment.

Try typing 3, 18, 30 and either Σ+ or DATA after each number. Then press the $\bar{x}$ key. You should see 17, which is the mean of 3, 18 and 30.

Note: Some calculators count the data as you enter it. Your calculator is one of these if it displayed 1 after you pressed 3, and then 2 after you pressed 18.

Note: To use the DATA button, you may need to put your calculator in STAT mode.

An ordinary scientific calculator cannot find the median or mode of a set of data; however, if it has the capability of finding the mean, it will count data and find its sum.

With a spreadsheet

Spreadsheets can find the mean of data in two ways. After numbers are typed in a list, they can be added and then divided as usual, or you can use the special average function to find the mean.

Example 3

Find the mean of the following numbers using a spreadsheet:

32   16   25   41

In Clarisworks:

Enter the numbers in cells A1 to A4, then type **=average(A1..A4)** *in cell A5. When the enter key is pressed, the average will be in cell A5.*

	A	B
1	32	
2	16	
3	25	
4	41	
5	=average(A1..A4)	

	A	B
1	32	
2	16	
3	25	
4	41	
5	28.5	

In Microsoft Excel, the command is: **=average(A1:A4)**

Some spreadsheets have commands to find the median and the mode of data.

In Microsoft Excel:

=median(A1:A4) returns the middle value of the numbers listed in cells A1 to A4.

=mode(B2:B25) returns the mode of the values listed in cells B2 to B25.

Some spreadsheets will also find the quartiles. In Microsoft Excel the command:

=quartile(A1:A24,1) will give the first, or lower quartile of the data in A1 to A24.

=quartile(A1:A24,3) will return the third, or upper quartile.

Sophisticated graphics calculators will construct box-and-whisker plots in which a moving cursor identifies the quartiles and the extreme values.

STANDARD DEVIATION

Using a calculator or a computer program to find the standard deviation is easy but often confusing since there are usually two forms, one for a sample and one for a population.

On a calculator

Most scientific calculators have both σ_n and σ_{n-1}.

- σ_n is the standard deviation for an entire population. It is calculated by the formula:

$$s = \sqrt{\frac{\left(\Sigma x^2\right) - n\bar{x}^2}{n}}$$

- σ_{n-1} is the standard deviation for a sample of the population. It is calculated by the formula:

$$s = \sqrt{\frac{\left(\Sigma x^2\right) - n\bar{x}^2}{n(n-1)}}$$

which uses the nonbiased or $n - 1$ method.

High-school texts calculate the standard deviation using the formula for σ_n.

With a spreadsheet

In recent versions of Microsoft Excel, there are two commands for standard deviation:

- STDEV assumes that the data represents a sample of the population. It is related to σ_{n-1} on a calculator.
- STDEVP assumes that your data represents the entire population and gives the same result as σ_n on a calculator.

To conform to your textbook, use STDEVP.

In Clarisworks there is only one command for standard deviation, STDEV which is related to σ_{n-1} on the calculator.

Example 4

Find the standard deviation for the data 32, 56, 38, 23, 34.5 and 62:

a) using a scientific calculator

b) using a spreadsheet program

a) *Put the calculator in STAT mode if necessary and enter the data. Press the σ_n key, using the shift or 2nd function key if necessary. Your answer should be 13.67.*

b) *Enter the data in cells A1 to A6 as shown.*

In cell A7, type **=STDEVP (A1:A6)** *or the appropriate command for your spreadsheet. When the enter key is pressed, the answer 13.67 will appear in A7.*

	A	B
1	32	
2	16	
3	25	
4	41	
5	34.5	
6	62	
7	=STDEVP(A1:A6)	

Try changing one of the values and watch the standard deviation change!

Remember that the standard deviation is a measure of spread. The average of the data in example 4 is 35.1. According to Chebyshev's theorem, when k = 2, at least $\frac{3}{4}$ of the data lies within 2 standard deviations of the mean. In this case σ = 13.67 and 2 standard deviations are 27.34. Therefore, we know that **at least** $\frac{3}{4}$ of the data will lie between 7.76 and 62.44. In this case, **all the data** lies in that region.

DESCRIPTIVE STATISTICS

The mean, median, mode and standard deviation are examples of descriptive statistics. They describe the features of the data set. Some calculators and spreadsheets will provide a list of descriptive statistics for a selected set of data. For example, the most common descriptive statistics for the data 8, 17, 9, 21, 17 are:

$\bar{x} = 14.4$	the mean $\bar{x}$
$\sum x = 72$	the sum $\sum x$
$\sum x^2 = 1164$	the sum of squares $\sum x^2$
$Sx = 5.639148872$	the sample standard deviation (σ_{n-1}) Sx
$\sigma x = 5.043808085$	the population standard deviation (σ_n) σx
$n = 5$	and the number of data n

Each item on this list can be displayed individually on most scientific calculators. Experiment by entering the values 8, 17, 9, 21 and 17 and searching the buttons on your calculator for the symbols in the list.

THE NORMAL DISTRIBUTION

On a calculator

A scientific calculator cannot display the curve of the distribution nor calculate the values of the areas under the curve.

A graphics calculator can graph the normal curve if the equation $y = \frac{1}{\sigma\sqrt{2\pi}} e^{\frac{-1}{2}\left(\frac{x-\mu}{\sigma}\right)^2}$ is entered, using numerical values for μ and σ.

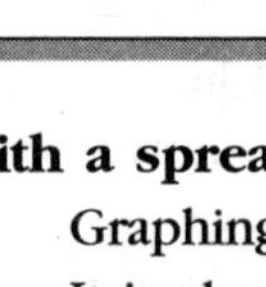

For students who have studied calculus:
If a calculator is able to evaluate definite integrals, the values in the table of areas can be produced by writing a program to find the area under the normal curve N(0,1) from 0 to a particular z value.

With a spreadsheet

Graphing the normal curve:

It is clumsy to enter the equation for the normal distribution in a spreadsheet, but it can be done.

- In cell A1 enter –4.0 and in A2 enter = **A1 + 0.2**. Use the Fill Down command to extend the list in column A to 4.0 (Using = **A1 + 0.5** will produce a shorter list but the curve will be smoother if more points are plotted.)

- Choose values for μ and σ. Example: Let $\mu = 50$ and let $\sigma = 2$.
- In cell B1 enter $\frac{1}{\sigma\sqrt{2\pi}} e^{\frac{-1}{2}\left(\frac{x-\mu}{\sigma}\right)^2}$ using the values 50 and 2 for the mean and the standard deviation, and substituting A1 for x. The expression might look like this:

  =1/(50*SQRT(2*PI))(EXP(-0.5((A1-50)/2)^2))

* You can type the numerical approximations 2.718 for e and 3.1416 for π but many spreadsheets have built in values for these numbers. They are often abbreviated EXP and PI.

- Once the expression is entered, use Fill Down to evaluate for all elements in column A.
- Graph the curve by selecting the two columns and choosing a line graph.

Finding areas under the normal curve:

Some spreadsheets have a function that returns the values of the areas under the normal curve $N(0,1)$. For example, in Microsoft Excel the command NORMSDIST(1.3333) gives the value 0.9088 which is the area under the normal curve $N(0,1)$ to the left of 1.333. Some also have a function to standardize a variable, given the mean and standard deviation.

TWO VARIABLE STATISTICS

Scatterplots on a calculator

An ordinary scientific calculator will not display a scatterplot but a graphics calculator will. Enter the first element in the ordered pair as an x value and the second element as a y value. Select the menu item that produces a scatterplot. If the points are not within view, alter the range settings for the screen display.

Scatterplots on a spreadsheet

All spreadsheets will produce scatterplots. Even such programs as MSWorks for DOS will take data entered in columns and display it as points on a grid.

A spreadsheet will normally plot a column of data as a set of points by associating the numbers with the numbers 1, 2, 3... on the horizontal axis. If there are two columns of numbers, the program assumes that each column represents a set to be plotted and it will graph both sets (usually in different colors). In order to produce a scatter diagram, the first column must be defined as x data, that is, the values to be used on the x axis.

Finding the line or curve of best fit

All graphics calculators can perform linear regression procedures. This means that they use the method of least squares to calculate and plot the line of best fit. If data are not related in a linear way - that is, a straight line does not represent the data accurately, most have other built-in regression procedures. For example, the TI-81 will produce the constants for linear, logarithmic, exponential and power regressions.

Simple spreadsheets such as MSWorks for DOS will not fit a line to data. More sophisticated spreadsheets such as Microsoft Excel and Quattro Pro have a command that will plot the line of best fit.

In addition, when a scatterplot is selected, some spreadsheets will display the equation.

Example 5

Mr. Scott gave his class a math test with two sections, A and B, that had questions of similar difficulty. In section A students were allowed to use calculators and in section B they were not allowed to use them. He recorded a mark out of 100 for each section as shown.

Name	A	B	Name	A	B	Name	A	B
Martha	92	88	Sharon	80	78	Niko	83	87
Paul	65	68	Ashantha	78	84	Jessica	77	77
Natya	73	70	David	50	36	Nareg	94	100
Samuel	85	72	Ivy	96	98	Rhodri	80	83
George	68	55	Jean	87	85	Mike	52	48
Frieda	54	42	Brandon	62	60	Dija	71	75
Arjun	79	82	Emily	65	61	Sarah	76	70
May	98	98	Ola	76	68	Amy	53	54

Find the line or curve of best fit for the data:

a) using a graphics calculator

b) using a spreadsheet such as Microsoft Excel

a) *Enter the data into the calculator and display a scatterplot.*

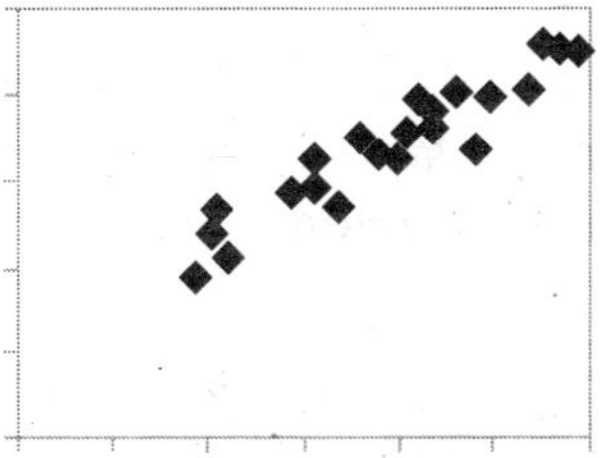

**If the plot doesn't appear, you may have to adjust the minimum and maximum x and y values.*

This plot displays x values from 40 to 100 and y values from 0 to 100.

The plot shows a positive correlation. Students' marks in the two sections were closely related. If they got a high mark in section A, they also got a high mark in section B.

It appears that a straight line would fit the plot best but we don't need to guess. A graphics calculator will perform a linear regression to work out the values of a and b for the linear equation y = bx + a and will then tell us how good an approximation that line will be. It does this by calculating the **correlation coefficient**.

The **correlation coefficient** measures how close the points are to the straight line. It is symbolized by r. If r is 1 or -1, the data fits the line perfectly. If r is close to 0, either positively or negatively, the line is not a good approximation. The sign (+ or -) tells us if the correlation is positive or negative.

After carrying out the linear regression, the calculator will display a list similar to the following:

a = – 14.88492283 **b = 1.168471654** **r = .9457829941**	**a** *and* **b** *are the constants for the linear equation and* **r** *is the correlation coefficient.*

From this list we know that the line of best fit has equation $y = 1.1685x - 14.885$ *and since the value of* **r** *is close to 1, the line is a good match for the data.*

A graphics calculator will display this equation and graph the line. For example, using the TI-81:

- *To display the equation of the line of best fit: choose* **VARS**, **LR** *and then* **RegEQ**.
- *To graph the line of best fit: press* **Y=** *to enter an equation, then choose* **VARS**, **LR** *and then* **RegEQ**. *The equation can now be plotted by pressing* **GRAPH**. *To display the scatterplot as well, choose* **Scatter** *as before under the* **DRAW** *menu.*

Notice that the equation used in linear regression is $y = bx + a$. This is a little confusing since $y = mx + b$ is a more familiar representation for the general linear equation.

Try experimenting with the other regressions available. Most graphics calculators have options for fitting a logarithmic curve, exponential curve or power curve to the data. They also display values of **a**, **b** and **r**. Below are the results for example 5.

Regression	Equation	Values for Example 5
Logarithmic	$y = b\ln x + a$	a = –284.66, b = 83.12, r = .945
Exponential	$y = ab^x$	a = 18.92, b = 1.02, r = .927
Power	$y = ax^b$	a = .306, b = 1.27, r = .94

The calculator will not take into account the fact that a point may be an outlier. It is important to eliminate such a point to get a line or curve that accurately summarizes the data.

b) *In Microsoft Excel or Quattro Pro, enter the data in two rows. Select the data and create a scatterplot, altering the axis values and entering labels as desired.*

After selecting the scatterplot, choose the command to insert a line or curve of best fit (sometimes called a trendline).

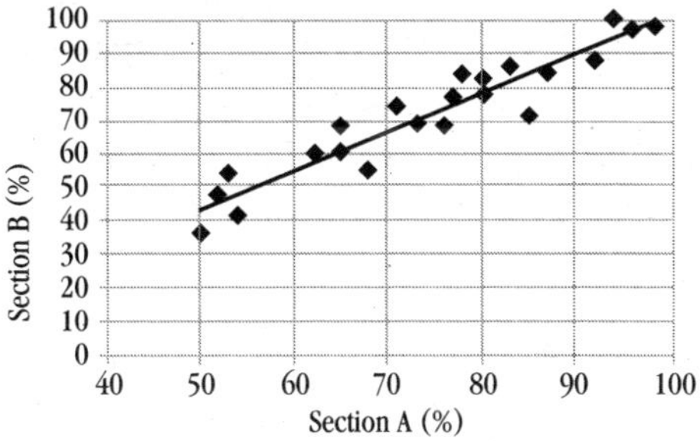

Most spreadsheets will provide the following options for regression:

linear, logarithmic, power, exponential and polynomial.

Note: If you select a polynomial regression you must choose the degree. For example, if you'd like a quadratic curve, you would pick degree 2.

Solutions to practice exercises

PRACTICE EXERCISE CHAPTER 1

1. a) Survey a random sample of car owners to calculate the percentage who have had cars stolen. Then survey car owners who have the passive device installed.
   b) Use records kept at the stadium to calculate the average attendance for last season.
   c) Using information on frequency of arrivals and departures, conduct a simulation to analyze the need for another runway.

2. A random sample is a sample in which each member of the population has an equal chance of being selected. It is used to avoid bias in the results.

3 Melanie could put all 1000 names in a hat and draw 40, or she could choose every 25th name in the school's list of students. (There are other possible answers.)

4. a) Assign each household a number between 0 and 399. Then, using a table of 3-digit random numbers, start anywhere on the page and proceed from there, circling any number that corresponds to a household number until 50 have been chosen.
   b) Assign each household a number between 0.000 and 0.399. Using the random feature on the calculator, generate numbers and write down any that correspond to a household number until 50 have been selected.

5. a) Since there are 12 months, any experiment that results in 12 different possibilities can be used in the simulation. For example: There are 12 possibilities when tossing a coin and rolling a die. Drawing a tag from a hat containing 12 numbered tags also simulates the correct probability.

b) Leila can use each of the possibilities to represent a month. For example: Using a coin and a die, she could represent January by heads and a 1. She would then roll the coin and die 4 times and record the results.

6. a)

Hours worked per week	Tally	Frequency
None	✓ ✓ ✓ ✓ ✓ ✓ ✓ ✓ ✓ ✓ ✓ ✓ ✓ ✓ ✓ ✓	16
Less than 5	✓ ✓ ✓ ✓ ✓ ✓ ✓ ✓ ✓ ✓	10
5 to 10	✓ ✓ ✓ ✓ ✓ ✓ ✓ ✓ ✓ ✓ ✓ ✓ ✓ ✓	14
10 to 15	✓ ✓ ✓ ✓ ✓ ✓ ✓ ✓	8
More than 15	✓ ✓	2

b) $\frac{16}{50} = 0.32 = 32\%$, $\frac{10}{50} = 20\%$, $\frac{14}{50} = 28\%$, $\frac{8}{50} = 16\%$, $\frac{2}{50} = 4\%$

c) 12 000 (since 4% of 300 000 is 12 000)

PRACTICE EXERCISE CHAPTER 2

1. a) 10 intervals of 25 were used to group the data

Intervals	Tally	Frequency
200-225	|	1
225-250	|||	3
250-275	||	2
275-300	||||	4
300-325	~~||||~~	5
325-350	~~||||~~ |	6
350-375	||	2
375-400	|||	3
400-425	|||	3
425-450	|	1

b) The smallest value is 200 and the largest, 449. The 250 values were displayed using 10 intervals of 25.

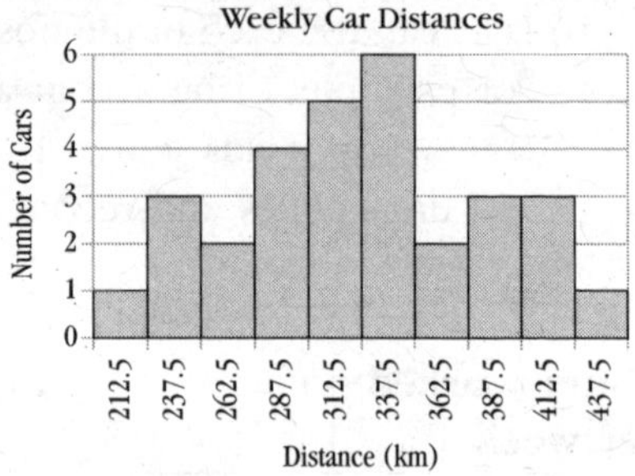

2. a) Circle graph
b) Pictograph
c) Broken line graph
d) Bar graph

3.

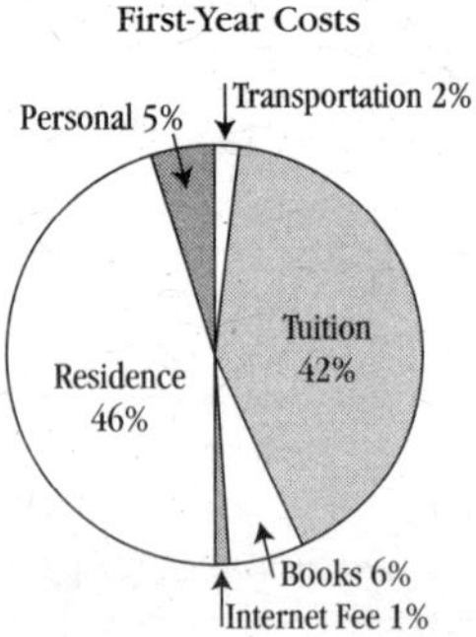

4. The vertical axis begins at 100 000 instead of zero and gives the impression that sales growth has been outstanding, when it has only been moderate.

5. From the graph, Green's can see an increase in CD sales and a decline in the sales of tapes. Marketing, advertising and stocking decisions will be affected by this picture.

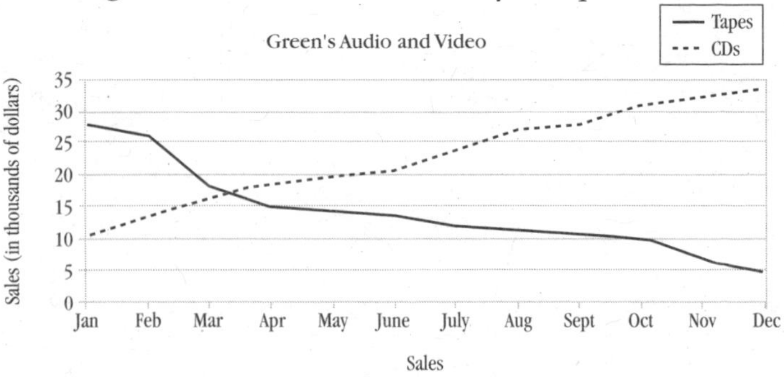

6.

4	7
5	3 7
6	3 6 0 8 5
7	4 5 1 7 9 3 7
8	4 5 5 3 8 6
9	2 0 8

PRACTICE EXERCISE CHAPTER 3

1. a) mean 5.6; median 5.5; modes 3 and 8
   b) mean \$3.69; median \$3.55; mode \$2.35
   c) This is categorical data. It does not make sense to talk about the mean language, or the median of French and Spanish. The modal language is English.

2. a) 20.5 b) 19
   c)

Interval	Frequency
0.5-4.5	2
4.5-8.5	5
8.5-12.5	4
12.5-16.5	5
16.5-20.5	7
20.5-24.5	5
24.5-28.5	5
28.5-32.5	3
32.5-36.5	2
36.5-40.5	2
40.5-44.5	1
44.5-48.5	1

d)

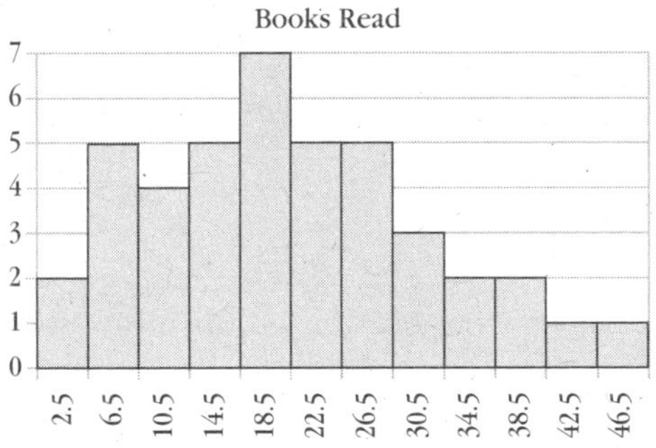

e) The median. The mean of 20.5 books is a little high. It does not reflect the large number of students who read very few books.

3. 84%

4. a) the mean kWh use per household for one month
   b) the mode of hat sizes
   c) the median income

5. Negatively skewed. The mean will be higher than the median.

PRACTICE EXERCISE CHAPTER 4

1. 9 (highest value = 12, lowest value = 3)

2. a) $\frac{24+1}{4} = 6.25 \rightarrow Q_L$ is the 7th value, which is 2

   $3\left(\frac{24+1}{4}\right) = 18.75 \rightarrow Q_U$ is the 18th value, which is 5

   The interquartile range is: $Q_U - Q_L = 5 - 2 = 3$

   b)

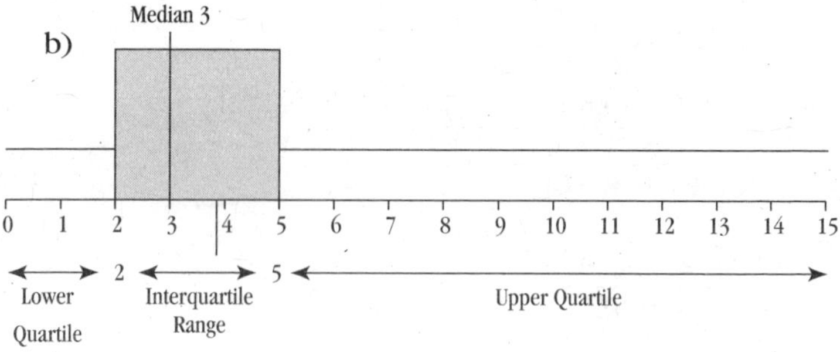

   c) An outlier is a value whose distance from the lower or upper quartile is more than 1.5 times the interquartile range. Since 1.5(3) = 4.5, any value less than –2.5 or greater than 9.5 is an outlier. Therefore, only 15 is an outlier.

3. 21.76

4. $14.50

5. 6.35 (Remember to use the group mean, which is 37.315.)

6. Between 38.5 and 48.5

PRACTICE EXERCISE CHAPTER 5

1. a) 20.25 b) $N(61.7, 5.3)$
   c) Symmetric about the mean, bell-shaped, area under the curve is 1 (other answers possible)
   d) The random variable X is normally distributed with mean 32 and variance 1.6.

2. a) $P(X < 0.85) = P(X < 0) + P(0 < X < 0.85)$
   $= 0.5 + 0.3023 = 0.8023$
   b) $P(X > 1.8) = P(X > 0) - P(0 < X < 1.8)$
   $= 0.5 - 0.4641 = 0.0359$
   c) $P(X > -2.1) = P(X < 2.1) = P(X < 0) + P(0 < X < 2.1)$
   $= 0.5 + 0.4821 = 0.9821$
   d) $P(-1.2 < X < 0.64) = P(X < 0.64) - P(X < -1.2)$
   $= 0.7389 - 0.1151 = 0.6238$

3. a) $P(X < 25) = P(Z < -1.11) = 0.1335$
   b) $P(X > 32.5) = P(Z > 0.56) = 0.5 - P(0 < Z < 0.56)$
   $= 0.5 - 0.2123 = 0.2877$
   c) $P(X > 28) \approx P(Z > -0.44) = P(Z < 0.44)$
   $= P(Z < 0) + P(0 < Z < 0.44)$
   $= 0.5 + 0.1700 = 0.6700$
   d) $P(26 < X < 35) = P(X < 35) - P(X < 26)$
   $= P(Z < 1.11) - P(Z < -0.89)$
   $= 0.8665 - 0.1867 = 0.6798$

4. 27 and 43

5. a) $P(X > 45) = 0.38, \therefore P(\mu < X < 45) = 0.12,$
   but $P(0 < Z < 0.31) = 0.12$
   also, $P(X > 52)$
   $= 0.14, \therefore P(\mu < X < 52) = 0.36,$ *but* $P(0 < Z < 1.08)$
   $= 0.36$

   Therefore, we can solve the two equations $45 = 0.3\sigma + \mu$ and $52 = 1.08\sigma + \mu$ to obtain $\mu = 42.3, \sigma = 9.0$

   b) $P(X < 40) = P(Z < -0.2555) = 0.3993$

6. $X \sim N(30, 6.25)$, therefore:
   $P(X > 32) = P(Z > 0.80) = P(Z > 0) - P(0 < Z < 0.80)$
   $= 0.5 - 0.2881 = 0.2119$

7. $X \sim N(750, 0.0001)$, therefore:

$P(749.99 < X < 750.02) = P(X < 750.02) - P(X < 749.99)$
$= P(Z < 2) - P(Z < -1) = 0.9772 - 0.1587 = 0.8185$

8. We need to find n such that $P(X < n) = 0.9$

$$P(Z < 1.28) = 0.9 \quad \therefore 1.28 = \frac{X - 28}{9} \rightarrow X = 39.52$$

and $P(X < 39.52) = 0.9$

Since there are 800 children, they should order 39.52(800) = 31 616 chocolate bars.

PRACTICE EXERCISE CHAPTER 6

1. Only a) and c)

In a) there are 2 possibilities - scoring and not scoring. Each attempt is independent and identical. In c) there are 2 possibilities - rolling a 2 or not rolling a 2. Each roll is independent and identical. In b) there are 3 possibilities - drawing a king, drawing an ace or drawing another card.

2. a) Success 0.5, failure 0.5 (There are 3 even numbers and 3 odd numbers on a die.)

b) Success 0.0769, failure 0.9231 (There are 4 kings in a deck.)

c) Success 0.143, failure 0.857 (Sunday is 1 out of 7 possible days.)

3 a) The probability distribution for Brian's 4 times at bat, where p(2) is the probability that he will get 2 hits in 4 times at bat:

$$p(0) = \binom{4}{0}\left(\frac{1}{4}\right)^0\left(\frac{3}{4}\right)^{4-0} = \binom{4}{0}\left(\frac{1}{4}\right)^0\left(\frac{3}{4}\right)^4 = 1(1)\left(\frac{81}{256}\right) = \frac{81}{256}$$

$$p(1) = \binom{4}{1}\left(\frac{1}{4}\right)^1\left(\frac{3}{4}\right)^{4-1} = \binom{4}{1}\left(\frac{1}{4}\right)^1\left(\frac{3}{4}\right)^3 = 4\left(\frac{1}{4}\right)\left(\frac{27}{64}\right) = \frac{27}{64}$$

$$p(2) = \binom{4}{2}\left(\frac{1}{4}\right)^2\left(\frac{3}{4}\right)^{4-2} = \binom{4}{2}\left(\frac{1}{4}\right)^2\left(\frac{3}{4}\right)^2 = 6\left(\frac{1}{16}\right)\left(\frac{9}{16}\right) = \frac{27}{128}$$

$$p(3) = \binom{4}{3}\left(\frac{1}{4}\right)^3\left(\frac{3}{4}\right)^{4-3} = \binom{4}{3}\left(\frac{1}{4}\right)^3\left(\frac{3}{4}\right)^1 = 4\left(\frac{1}{64}\right)\left(\frac{3}{4}\right) = \frac{3}{64}$$

$$p(4) = \binom{4}{4}\left(\frac{1}{4}\right)^4\left(\frac{3}{4}\right)^{4-4} = \binom{4}{4}\left(\frac{1}{4}\right)^4\left(\frac{3}{4}\right)^0 = 1\left(\frac{1}{256}\right)(1) = \frac{1}{256}$$

b) The probability distribution graph is approximately bell-shaped. It is skewed to the right.

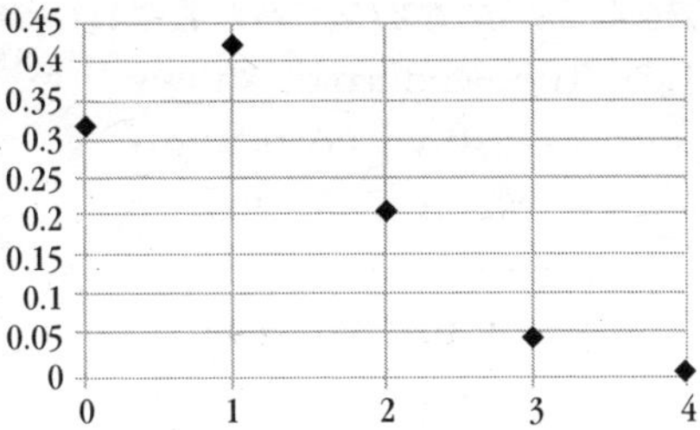

4 a) $np = 54.6$ $nq = 29.4$. Since they are both larger than 5, the distribution can be approximated by the normal distribution. Approximate mean is $\mu = np = 54.6$. Approximate variance is $\sigma^2 = npq = 54.6(0.35) = 19.11$

b) $np = 2.8$ $nq = 5.2$. Since np is less than 5 the distribution cannot be approximated by the normal distribution.

5. $p = 0.03$, $np = 200(0.03) = 6$, nq=$200(0.97) = 194$. Therefore, we can use a normal distribution with approximate mean $\mu = np = 6$ and variance $\sigma^2 = npq = 6(0.97) = 5.82$.
$P(X < 4) = P(X < 3.5) = P(Z < -1.036)$
$= 1 - P(Z < 1.036) = 1 - 0.8485 = 0.1515$
The probability that fewer than 4 handles are defective is approximately 15.15%.

6. $P(success) = p = \frac{1}{3}$ $P(failure) = q = \frac{2}{3}$; $np = 30\left(\frac{1}{3}\right) = 10, nq$

$= 30\left(\frac{2}{3}\right) = 20$; $\mu = np = 10$, $\sigma^2 = npq = 10\left(\frac{2}{3}\right) = \frac{20}{3} \approx 6.67$;

$P(X = 15) = P(14.5 \leq X \leq 15.5) = P(1.74 \leq Z \leq 2.13)$
$= P(Z \leq 2.13) - P(Z \leq 1.74) = 0.9834 - 0.9591 = 0.0243$
The probability of getting exactly 15 successes is 2.43%.

7. $p = 0.4$, $np = 50(0.4) = 20$, $nq = 50(0.6) = 30$,
$\therefore \mu = 20$ and $\sigma^2 = 12$
$P(X > 25) = P(X > 25.5) = P(Z > 1.59) = 1 - P(Z < 1.59)$
$= 1 - 0.9441 = 0.0559$
The probability that more than half the staff will catch the flu is approximately 5.6%.

PRACTICE EXERCISE CHAPTER 7

1. The scatterplot shows a positive correlation between total capacity and predicted electricity use per year.

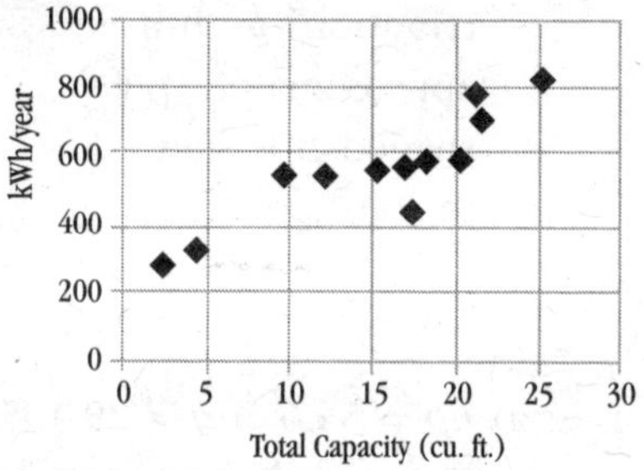

2. The scatterplot shows a positive correlation between yearly family income and graduation averages for the students; however, we cannot infer that giving families money will increase the graduation averages of their children. There are other factors to consider. For example, heads of families with higher incomes may be more likely to have higher levels of education. This could be the contributing factor.

3. Two points on the graph are (1,11) and (12,1). From these two points the slope m and the equation are calculated as follows:

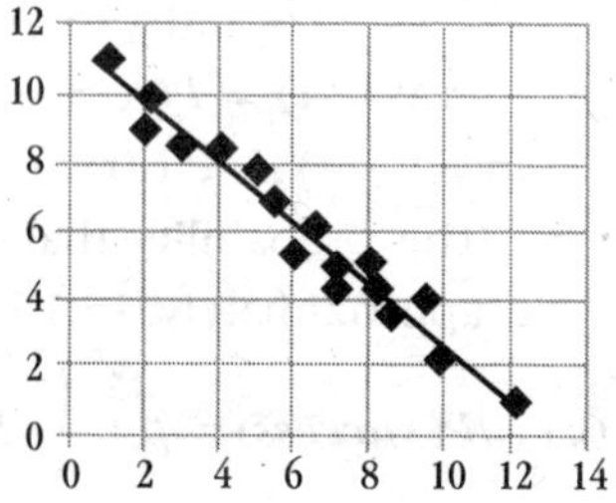

$$m = \frac{1-11}{12-1} \quad \therefore y - 11 = \frac{-10}{11}(x-1)$$
$$\therefore 11y - 121 = -10x + 10$$
$$\therefore 10x + 11y - 131 = 0$$

4. The sketched curve of best fit has the appearance of a logarithmic curve.

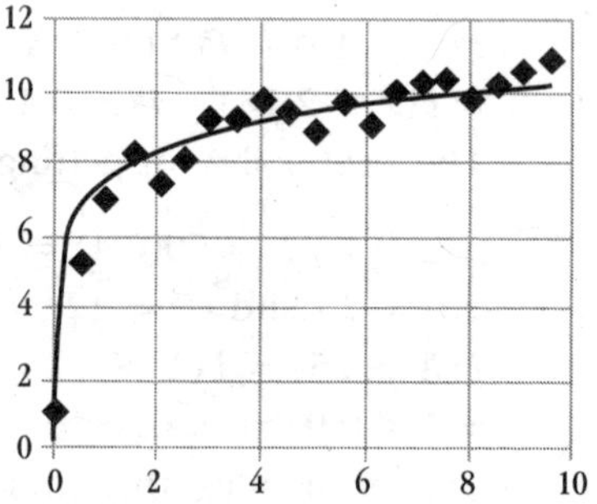

5. The first scatterplot shows a strong positive correlation and the second shows a weak negative correlation.

Sample statistics examination

Instructions

1. Provide complete solutions for each of the following questions.
2. Calculators are permitted.
3. Time allotted: 2 hours

1. Josh and Amy want the cafeteria at Riverview High to offer vegetarian food. Before approaching the principal, they decide to survey a sample of 40 students out of the school population of 950 to find out how many want a vegetarian menu. They go to Fred's Veggie Café, a favorite hang-out for Riverview students, and hand out 40 questionnaires.
   a) Explain why their survey method is flawed.
   b) Suggest two possible alternatives for improving their survey.
   c) Describe how they could use random numbers to select their sample.

2. Highway workers are planting ash, maple and oak trees along the roads. The seedlings are in mixed bags. Gord Francis, in charge of the project, wants to know how likely it is that more than 3 trees of the same type will be planted side by side. He decides to simulate the problem.
   a) What can he use in a simulation that will have the same probability as this event?
   b) Describe how he would carry out the simulation.

3. The following information was gathered from 40 high-school students in a survey to investigate the number of hours per

week spent on athletic activities, including those not related to school.

- 8 students did not participate in any athletic endeavor
- 14 students participated less than 5 hours a week
- 10 students participated between 5 and 10 hours a week
- 6 students participated between 10 and 15 hours a week
- 2 student participated more than 15 hours a week

a) Set up a tally sheet to display the information.

b) Calculate the percentage of students in each category.

c) Based on this study predict the number of students in a group of 450 000 who would not participate in any athletic activities.

4 At the Roosen yearly fishing derby, a group of eager 10-year-olds brought in 36 fish. The weights (in kg) are listed in the chart.

1.5	2.3	5.1	2.8	1.7	6.3	3.4	1.2	1.6	2.7	2.1	3.5
4.6	3.4	4.5	2.5	3.9	4.6	5.2	3.5	1.8	5.8	4.0	2.3
1.2	3.1	4.6	5.1	1.4	1.9	3.2	4.4	1.8	3.2	4.8	3.0

a) Organize the data in a frequency table.

b) Display the data in a histogram.

c) Find the mean, median and mode of the data.

5. Mitey Corporation presented this graph of its yearly expenditures to its shareholders:

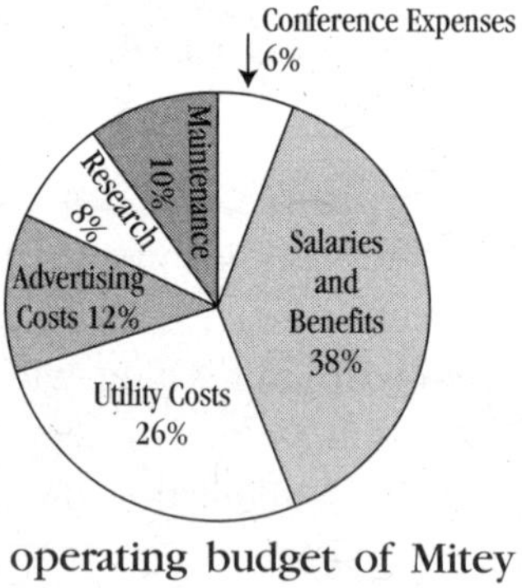

a) If the total operating budget of Mitey Corp. is $892 000, how much was spent on salaries and benefits?

b) How many degrees were used to construct the conference expenses section?

6. The biology class at Forest Heights school is following the growth of 24 goldfish in a new pond constructed in the school quadrangle. The following chart records the lengths (in cm) of the goldfish in September:

5.8	4.7	3.8	6.5	5.5	7.8	7.4	6.9	4.2	6.5	4.9	5.7
6.3	7.3	5.2	6.6	4.3	3.8	5.9	6.2	4.0	7.1	8.4	3.4

a) Display this data in a stem and leaf plot.
b) Find the mean of the goldfish lengths.
c) Find the standard deviation of the goldfish lengths.

7. Peter has an average of 83% in 7 subjects. What mark must he get in his 8th subject to raise his average to 85%?

8. In a ladies open golf tournament, 12 women had the following scores:

Ellen	Tanya	Pat	Lucy	Dora	Rose	Lyn	Sue	Barb	Gayle	Allie	Pam
106	94	90	93	102	99	128	89	92	109	96	105

a) Calculate the range of the data.
b) Determine the interquartile range.
c) Display the data in a box-and-whisker plot.
d) Identify any outliers in the data.

9. The table represents the monthly salaries of 30 employees of Arco Computer Industries. Find the standard deviation for this grouped data.

Intervals	**Frequency**
$1500 to 2500	4
$2500 to 3500	10
$3500 to 4500	8
$4500 to 5500	5
$5500 to 6500	2
$6500 to 7500	1

10. a) State the variance for data whose standard deviation is 2.6.
b) Write the notation for a normal distribution whose mean is 15.5 and standard deviation is 3.2.
c) If data is normally distributed with mean 51 and standard deviation 6.5, between what two values does 68% of the data lie?

11. If a random variable X is distributed normally with mean 0 and standard deviation 1, find:
a) the probability that $X < 0.75$
b) $P(X > -2.4)$
c) $P(-1.4 < X < 0.74)$

12. If a random variable $X \sim N(120, 42)$, find:
a) the probability that $X < 115$
b) $P(X > 131)$
c) $P(118 < X < 125)$

13. If $P(X > 112) = 0.58$ and $P(X > 130) = 0.14$, find:
a) the mean and the standard deviation
b) $P(X < 100)$

14. Assume that the amount of cheese on a large pizza from Frank's Pizzeria is normally distributed with mean 200 g and variance 25. Find the probability that, on inspection, the amount of cheese on a large pizza will be within the permissible limits of 195 g and 210 g.

15. A die is thrown 40 times. If a success is defined as rolling a 4 or a 5, determine the probability of getting exactly 15 successes in the 40 trials by using the normal approximation of the binomial distribution.

16. Draw an eyeball-fit line for the scatterplot and, using 2 points, find an equation for the line.

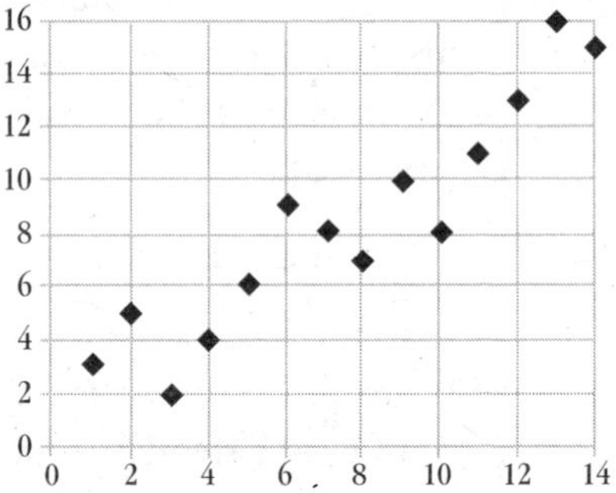

Solutions to sample examination

1. a) Josh and Amy's sample is flawed because it was not randomly chosen. Each member of the school population did not have the same chance of being surveyed. Students who do not like vegetarian food would not frequent the café. Thus the sample is biased in favor of those who are vegetarians or at least enjoy vegetarian food.

   b) They can put all 950 names in a hat and draw 40 to interview, or they can use random numbers to choose a sample of 40 students.

   c) To use random numbers they would assign a 3-digit number to each student. Then, using a table of 3-digit random numbers or the random feature on a calculator, they would write down the first 40 3-digit numbers that corresponded to a student at Riverview. Those students would be interviewed.

2. a) Since there are 3 types of trees, Gord needs to use something that has 3 possible outcomes. He could use a spinner with 3 equal sections, or he could use a 6-sided die and assign 2 numbers to each possibility, e.g., 1 and 4 to ash, 2 and 5 to maple, 3 and 6 to oak.

   b) If he used the spinner he would spin the arrow many times, writing down the results. He would then examine the list to count how frequently he had strings of more than 3 identical numbers.

3. a)

Hours spent on athletics per week	Tally	Frequency
None	✓ ✓ ✓ ✓ ✓ ✓ ✓ ✓	8
Less than 5	✓ ✓ ✓ ✓ ✓ ✓ ✓ ✓ ✓ ✓	14
	✓ ✓ ✓ ✓	
5 to 10	✓ ✓ ✓ ✓ ✓ ✓ ✓ ✓ ✓ ✓	10
10 to 15	✓ ✓ ✓ ✓ ✓ ✓	6
More than 15	✓ ✓	2

b) $\frac{8}{40} = 0.20 = 20\%, \frac{14}{40} = 35\%, \frac{10}{40} = 25\%, \frac{6}{40} = 15\%, \frac{2}{40} = 5\%$

Thus, 20% did no athletics, 35% spent less than 5 hours per week, 25% spent between 5 and 10 hours, 15% spent between 10 and 15 hours and 5% spent more than 15 hours.

c) 20% of 450 000 = 90 000. Therefore, 90 000 students out of 450 000 would not participate in any athletic activity.

4.a)

Intervals	Tally	Frequency
1-2	𝍸 IIII	9
2-3	𝍸 I	6
3-4	𝍸 IIII	9
4-5	𝍸 II	7
5-6	IIII	4
6-7	I	1

b)

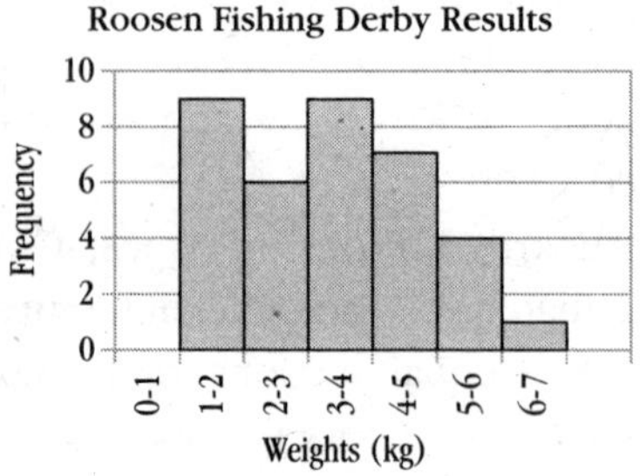

c) The mean is 3.28, found by adding all data values and dividing by 36. Since there are an even number of data values, there is no middle value. Thus, the median is the average of the 2 middle numbers. The 18th and 19th numbers are in the middle and both are 3.2. Therefore the median is 3.2.

The mode is 4.6 since there were more fish of this weight caught.

5. a) 38% of \$892 000 = 892 000 x 0.38 = 338 960. The amount spent on salaries and benefits was \$338 960.

b) The conference expenses section represents 6% of the circle: 6% of 360° = 0.06 x 360 = 21.6°

6. a)

3	4 8 8
4	0 2 3 7 9
5	2 5 7 8 9
6	2 3 5 5 6 9
7	1 3 4 8
8	4

b) The mean is: $\frac{\Sigma x}{n} = \frac{138.2}{24} \approx 5.76$

c) The standard deviation is:

$$\sigma = \sqrt{\frac{\Sigma fx^2 - n\bar{x}^2}{n}} = \sqrt{\frac{840.56 - 24(5.76)^2}{24}} = 1.3656 \text{ or}$$

approximately 1.4

7. Since Peter's average on 7 subjects is 83%, he has a total of 7(83) = 581 marks. In order to have an average of 85 in 8 subjects, he needs 8(85) = 680 marks. Thus he needs to get 99% in his 8th subject.

8. a) The range of the data is the difference between the highest and lowest values. The highest value is 128 and the lowest is 89. Therefore the range is 39.

b) Put the data in order:

89 90 92 93 94 96 99 102 105 106 109 128

- The lower quartile is at the $\frac{12+1}{4} = 3.25$ th position. Using the 4th piece of data to approximate Q_L gives a value of 93.
- The upper quartile is at the $3\left(\frac{12+1}{4}\right) = 9.75$th position. Using the 9th piece of data to approximate Q_U gives a value of 105.

Therefore, the interquartile range is: $Q_U - Q_L = 105 - 93 = 12$

c)

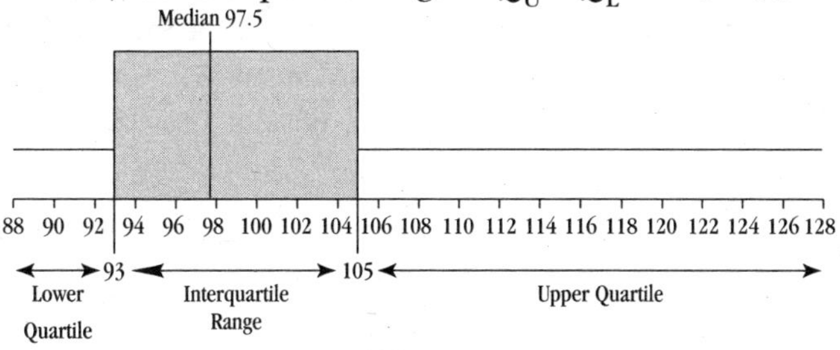

d) 1.5(12) = 18. Therefore, any data points further than 18 from the box are outliers.

Since 93 - 18 = 75 and 105 + 18 = 123, only 128 is an outlier in this data set.

9. The formula for the standard deviation of grouped data is:

$$s = \sqrt{\frac{\left(\Sigma x^2 f(x)\right) - n\bar{x}^2}{n}}$$

where x is the midpoint of an interval and $f(x)$ is the number of values in the interval.

Set up the table to calculate x, $f(x)$ and $x^2 f(x)$:

Intervals	x	$f(x)$	$x^2 f(x)$
$1500 to 2500	2000	4	16 000 000
$2500 to 3500	3000	10	90 000 000
$3500 to 4500	4000	8	128 000 000
$4500 to 5500	5000	5	125 000 000
$5500 to 6500	6000	2	72 000 000
$6500 to 7500	7000	1	49 000 000
		Sum	480 000 000

The mean

$$\bar{x} = \frac{4(2000) + 10(3000) + 8(4000) + 5(5000) + 2(6000) + 1(7000)}{30}$$

$$= 3800$$

Thus:

$$s = \sqrt{\frac{\left(\Sigma x^2 f(x)\right) - n\bar{x}^2}{n}} = \sqrt{\frac{480000000 - 30(3800)}{30}} = 3999.53$$

10. a) $\sigma = 2.6 \therefore \sigma^2 = 6.76$. Therefore, the variance is 6.76.

b) $N(15.5, 10.24)$

c) If data is normally distributed, 68% of the data lies within 1 standard deviation of the mean: 51 + 6.5 = 57.5 and 51 - 6.5 = 44.5. Therefore 68% of the data lies between 44.5 and 57.5.

11. Since the random variable X is distributed normally with mean 0 and standard deviation 1:

a) The probability that $X < 0.75$ is found by calculating $P(X < 0.75)$. From the tables:

$P(X < 0.75) = P(X < 0) + P(0 < X < 0.75)$

$= 0.5000 + 0.2734 = 0.7734$

b) $P(X > -2.4) = P(X < 2.4) = P(X < 0) + P(0 < X < 2.4)$

$= 0.5 + 0.4918 = 0.9918$

c) $P(-1.4 < X < 0.74) = P(X < 0.74) - P(X < -1.4)$

Consider $P(X < 0.74) = P(X < 0) + P(0 < X < 0.74)$

$= 0.5 + 0.2704 = 0.7704$

and $P(X < -1.4) = P(X > 1.4)$

$= 0.5 - P(0 < X < 1.4) = 0.5 - 0.4192 = 0.0808$

Therefore, $P(-1.4 < X < 0.74) = 0.7704 - 0.0808 = 0.6896$

12. Since X has distribution $N(120,42)$, it is necessary to standardize the variable before calculating the probabilities.

a) $Z = \dfrac{X - \bar{x}}{\sigma} = \dfrac{115 - 120}{\sqrt{42}} \approx -0.77$

Therefore, $P(X < 115) \approx P(Z < -0.77) = P(Z > 0.77)$

$= 0.5 - P(0 < Z < 0.77)$

$= 0.5 - 0.2794 = 0.2206$

b) $Z = \dfrac{X - \bar{x}}{\sigma} = \dfrac{131 - 120}{\sqrt{42}} \approx 1.70$

Therefore, $P(X > 131) \approx P(Z > 1.70)$

$= 0.5 - P(0 < Z < 1.70) = 0.5 - 0.4554 = 0.0446$

c) $Z_1 = \dfrac{X - \bar{x}}{\sigma} = \dfrac{118 - 120}{\sqrt{42}} \approx -0.31$ and $Z_2 = \dfrac{125 - 120}{\sqrt{42}} \approx 0.77$

Therefore, $P(118 < X < 125) \approx P(-0.31 < Z < 0.77)$

$= P(Z < 0.77) - P(Z < -0.31)$

but $P(Z < 0.77) = 0.5 + P(0 < Z < 0.77)$

$= 0.5 + 0.2794 = 0.7794$

and $P(Z < -0.31) = P(Z > 0.31) = 0.5 - P(0 < Z < 0.31)$

$= 0.5 - 0.1217 = 0.3783$

Therefore, $P(118 < X < 125) = 0.7794 - 0.3783 = 0.4011$

13. Since $P(X > 112) = 0.58$, then 112 is to the left of the mean.
Therefore, $P(112 < X < \mu) = 0.58 - 0.50 = 0.08$
From the table: $P(0 < Z < 0.20) = 0.08$.
Therefore, $P(-0.20 < Z < 0) = 0.08$
Thus, $X = 112 \rightarrow Z = -0.20$
Since $P(X > 130) = 0.14$, $P(\mu < X < 130) = 0.5 - 0.14 = 0.36$
From the table: $P(0 < Z < 1.08) = 0.36$.
Thus, $X = 130 \rightarrow Z = 1.08$

$X = 112$ and $Z = -0.20 \quad \rightarrow \quad 112 = -0.2\sigma + \mu$

$X = 130$ and $Z = 1.08 \quad \rightarrow \quad 130 = 1.08\sigma + \mu$

Subtracting $\rightarrow \quad 18 = 1.28\sigma$

$$\sigma = \frac{18}{1.28} = 14.0625$$

Substituting back in the first equation

$$\rightarrow 112 = -0.2(14.0625) + \mu$$

$$\mu = 114.8125$$

Therefore, the mean is 114.81 and the standard deviation is 14.06, correct to 2 decimal places.

b) $Z = \dfrac{100 - 114.81}{14.06} \approx -1.05$

Therefore $P(X < 100) = P(Z < -1.05) = P(Z > 1.05)$
$= P(Z > 0) - P(0 < Z < 1.05)$
$= 0.5 - 0.3531 = 0.1469$

14. We need to find $P(195 \leq X \leq 210)$ given that X is normally distributed with distribution $N(200,25)$.

If $X = 195 \rightarrow Z = \dfrac{195 - 200}{5} = -1$ and

If $X = 210 \rightarrow Z = \dfrac{210 - 200}{5} = 2$

Therefore, $P(195 < X < 210) = P(-1 < Z < 2)$
$P(-1 < Z < 2) = P(-1 < Z < 0) + P(0 < Z < 2)$
$= P(0 < Z < 1) + P(0 < Z < 2)$
$= 0.3413 + 0.4772 = 0.8185$

Thus, on inspection there is approximately an 81.85% chance that the amount of cheese falls within the acceptable limits.

15. $n = 40$, $p = \dfrac{1}{3}$ and $q = \dfrac{2}{3}$. Thus, $np = \dfrac{40}{3}$ and $nq = \dfrac{80}{3}$

Since np and nq are both larger than 5, we can use the binomial distribution.

The mean is $\mu = np = \frac{40}{3} = 13.3$ and the variance is

$$\sigma^2 = npq = \frac{40}{3}\left(\frac{2}{3}\right) = \frac{80}{9} = 8.9$$

$P(X = 15)$ in the binomial distribution is equivalent to $P(14.5 < X < 15.5)$ in the normal distribution.

If $X = 14.5 \rightarrow Z = \frac{14.5 - 13.3}{\sqrt{8.9}} \approx 0.40$

and if $X = 15.5 \rightarrow Z = \frac{15.5 - 13.3}{\sqrt{8.9}} \approx 0.74$

Thus, $P(14.5 < X < 15.5) = P(0.40 < Z < 0.74)$
$= P(0 < Z < 0.74) - P(0 < Z < 0.4)$
$= 0.2704 - 0.1554 = 0.115$

There is an 11.5% probability of getting exactly 15 successes out of 40 rolls.

16. The line is drawn so that as many points as possible fall on the line and approximately the same number of points are above the line as below.

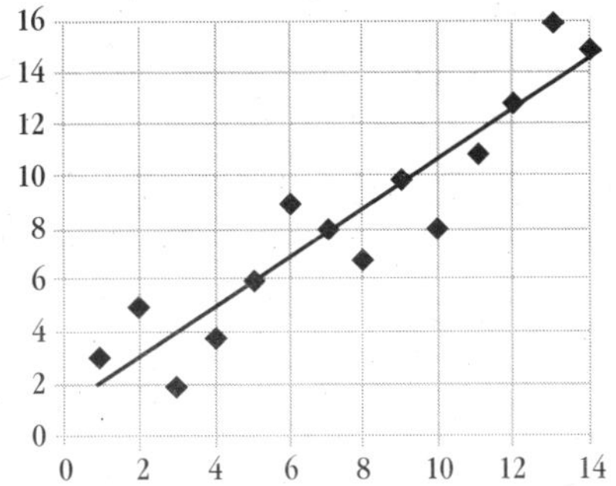

Answers may vary depending on the line drawn. Two points on the eyeball-fit line shown are (5,6) and (7,8). From these two points, the slope m and the equation are calculated as follows:

$$m = \frac{8-6}{7-5} = 1 \qquad \therefore y - 6 = 1(x - 5)$$

$$\therefore y - 6 = x - 5$$

$$\therefore x - y + 1 = 0$$

An equation for the line is

$$x - y + 1 = 0$$

Definitions and formulas

Area probability graph A graph that shows the **probability** of each result in an experiment. If the variable is discrete, the graph is made up of columns. The area of each column gives the probability of that result. If the data is continuous, the graph is a curve. The area under the curve between two values gives the probability that the variable lies in that region.

Binomial distribution The results of repeated experiments that are independent and identical and in which there are two possible outcomes each time.

Box-and-whisker plot A diagram that is used to illustrate the interquartile range. The "box" surrounds the middle two quartiles and the "whiskers" extend to the ends of the data.

Chebyshev's theorem At least $\left(1-\frac{1}{k^2}\right)$ of data lies within k standard deviations of the mean, where $k > 1$.

Correlation A relationship between two variables. If one variable increases as the other increases, the correlation is positive. If one variable decreases as the other increases, the correlation is negative.

Curve of best fit A curve that best summarizes the data in a particular scatterplot. It may be described by a polynomial, logarithmic, exponential or other equation.

Frequency distribution A table that displays an ordered set of values and the frequencies for each value.

Interquartile range The region covered by the two middle quartiles, or fourths, in a set of data.

Line of best fit A line drawn through a set of points that summarizes the data. An eyeball-fit line should be drawn so that it:

1. passes through as many points as possible, and
2. has approximately the same number of data points above and below.

Mean The average found by dividing the sum of all values in a set by the number of values in the set.

Mean deviation The average distance of the data values from the mean.

Median The middle value in a set of values that have been arranged from lowest to highest. If there is no middle value, the median is the average of the middle two values. Half the data lies above the median and half lies below.

Mode The value that occurs most often in a set of values. A set can have more than one mode.

Normal distribution The general normal distribution is described by $N(\mu, \sigma^2)$, where μ is the mean and σ is the standard deviation. It is used to analyze many real-life phenomena. Approximately 68% of the data lies within 1 standard deviation of the mean and 95% of the data within 2 standard deviations.

Outlier A value whose distance from the first or the third quartile is more than 1.5 times the interquartile range.

Population The whole group of people or things that is being studied.

Random sample A sample selected in such a way that every member of the population involved has an equal chance of being included.

Range The difference between the highest and lowest values in the sample.

Sample The part of the population on which information will actually be collected.

Simulation An experiment that has the same probability as the problem being investigated. A simulation is used when it is too time-consuming or difficult to gather results from a survey or observation.

Skewed A word used to describe a frequency distribution in which values are clustered at one end of the scale and spread out at the other. For example, a distribution that is high at the extreme left and trails off on the right side is said to be positively skewed.

Standard deviation The most often used measure of variability. In the normal distribution, the standard deviation represents the distance from the mean to the point of inflection of the curve. There are several abbreviations for standard deviation. Most books use SD or *s* to denote the standard deviation for a sample and σ (pronounced sigma),which is the lowercase Greek letter for *s* for the standard deviation of a population. Calculators often use σ_n and σ_{n-1} for the standard deviation.

Standardized variable In order to use an area table for normal curves to analyze distributions other than $N(0,1)$, it is necessary to *standardize* the random variable X. The letter Z is used for the standardized variable.

Stem and leaf plot A diagram that organizes data by listing it according to its digits. For example, if the data consists of 2-digit numbers, the 10s digit is the stem and the 1s digit is the leaf.

Table of random digits A table of numbers in columns, usually created by computer, that is used to choose a random sample.

Tally chart A table that is used to record and count data.

Variability The characteristic that describes how much the data is spread out from the mean.

Variance The square of the standard deviation. It is represented by σ^2.

Binomial Distribution

$p(x) = \binom{n}{x} p^x q^{n-x}$, where:

- $p(x)$ means the probability of x successes.
- $\binom{n}{x} = \frac{n!}{x!(n-x)!}$ is the number of ways of getting x successes in n trials
- p^x denotes the probability of x successes
- q^{n-x} denotes the probability of $n - x$ failures

Percent

To calculate a percent from a ratio	To calculate a percent of a total
$\frac{48}{128} \Rightarrow 48 \div 128 \times 100 = 37.5\%$	37.5% of $1200 \Rightarrow 1200 \times 0.375 = 450$

Means

- Mean of a *sample* of the population: $\bar{x} = \frac{\Sigma x}{n}$, where Σx is the sum of all the values in the sample and n is the number of values in the sample.
- Mean of grouped data: $\bar{x} = \frac{\Sigma x f(x)}{n}$ where $\Sigma x f(x)$ is the product of the different values and their frequencies.
- Weighted mean: $\bar{x} = \frac{\Sigma wx}{\Sigma w}$, where Σwx is the sum of the data multiplied by their weightings and Σw is the sum of the weightings.

Median

To find the median:

- Organize the data from smallest to largest.
- If there is an odd number of values, the median is the middle value.
- If there is an even number of values, the median is the average of the two middle values.

Mean deviation

$$\frac{\Sigma|x - \bar{x}|}{n}$$

Standard deviation

- Basic formula: $s = \sqrt{\dfrac{\Sigma(x - \bar{x})^2}{n}}$

- Formula for easier calculation: $s = \sqrt{\dfrac{\left(\Sigma x^2\right) - n\bar{x}^2}{n}}$

- Formula for grouped data: $s = \sqrt{\dfrac{\left(\Sigma x^2 f(x)\right) - n\bar{x}^2}{n}}$, where x is the midpoint of an interval and $f(x)$ is the number of values in the interval.

Standardizing a variable

$$Z = \frac{X - \mu}{\sigma}$$

Table of areas under the normal curve N(0,1)

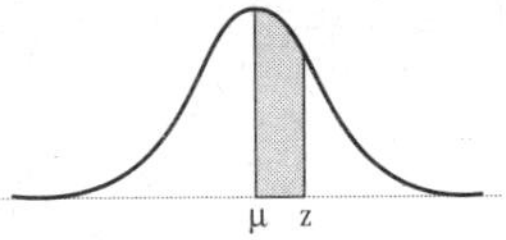

z	0.00	0.01	0.02	0.03	0.04	0.05	0.06	0.07	0.08	0.09
0.0	0.0000	0.0040	0.0080	0.0120	0.0160	0.0199	0.0239	0.0279	0.0319	0.0359
0.1	0.0398	0.0438	0.0478	0.0517	0.0557	0.0596	0.0636	0.0675	0.0714	0.0753
0.2	0.0793	0.0832	0.0871	0.0910	0.0948	0.0987	0.1026	0.1064	0.1103	0.1141
0.3	0.1179	0.1217	0.1255	0.1293	0.1331	0.1368	0.1406	0.1443	0.1480	0.1517
0.4	0.1554	0.1591	0.1628	0.1664	0.1700	0.1736	0.1772	0.1808	0.1844	0.1879
0.5	0.1915	0.1950	0.1985	0.2019	0.2054	0.2088	0.2123	0.2157	0.2190	0.2224
0.6	0.2257	0.2291	0.2324	0.2357	0.2389	0.2422	0.2454	0.2486	0.2517	0.2549
0.7	0.2580	0.2611	0.2642	0.2673	0.2704	0.2734	0.2764	0.2794	0.2823	0.2852
0.8	0.2881	0.2910	0.2939	0.2967	0.2995	0.3023	0.3051	0.3078	0.3106	0.3133
0.9	0.3159	0.3186	0.3212	0.3238	0.3264	0.3289	0.3315	0.3340	0.3365	0.3389
1.0	0.3413	0.3438	0.3461	0.3485	0.3508	0.3531	0.3554	0.3577	0.3599	0.3621
1.1	0.3643	0.3665	0.3686	0.3708	0.3729	0.3749	0.3770	0.3790	0.3810	0.3830
1.2	0.3849	0.3869	0.3888	0.3907	0.3925	0.3944	0.3962	0.3980	0.3997	0.4015
1.3	0.4032	0.4049	0.4066	0.4082	0.4099	0.4115	0.4131	0.4147	0.4162	0.4177
1.4	0.4192	0.4207	0.4222	0.4236	0.4251	0.4265	0.4279	0.4292	0.4306	0.4319
1.5	0.4332	0.4345	0.4357	0.4370	0.4382	0.4394	0.4406	0.4418	0.4429	0.4441
1.6	0.4452	0.4463	0.4474	0.4484	0.4495	0.4505	0.4515	0.4525	0.4535	0.4545
1.7	0.4554	0.4564	0.4573	0.4582	0.4591	0.4599	0.4608	0.4616	0.4625	0.4633
1.8	0.4641	0.4649	0.4656	0.4664	0.4671	0.4678	0.4686	0.4693	0.4699	0.4706
1.9	0.4713	0.4719	0.4726	0.4732	0.4738	0.4744	0.4750	0.4756	0.4761	0.4767
2.0	0.4772	0.4778	0.4783	0.4788	0.4793	0.4798	0.4803	0.4808	0.4812	0.4817
2.1	0.4821	0.4826	0.4830	0.4834	0.4838	0.4842	0.4846	0.4850	0.4854	0.4857
2.2	0.4861	0.4864	0.4868	0.4871	0.4875	0.4878	0.4881	0.4884	0.4887	0.4890
2.3	0.4893	0.4896	0.4898	0.4901	0.4904	0.4906	0.4909	0.4911	0.4913	0.4916
2.4	0.4918	0.4920	0.4922	0.4925	0.4927	0.4929	0.4931	0.4932	0.4934	0.4936
2.5	0.4938	0.4940	0.4941	0.4943	0.4945	0.4946	0.4948	0.4949	0.4951	0.4952
2.6	0.4953	0.4955	0.4956	0.4957	0.4959	0.4960	0.4961	0.4962	0.4963	0.4964
2.7	0.4965	0.4966	0.4967	0.4968	0.4969	0.4970	0.4971	0.4972	0.4973	0.4974
2.8	0.4974	0.4975	0.4976	0.4977	0.4977	0.4978	0.4979	0.4979	0.4980	0.4981
2.9	0.4981	0.4982	0.4982	0.4983	0.4984	0.4984	0.4985	0.4985	0.4986	0.4986
3.0	0.4987	0.4987	0.4987	0.4988	0.4988	0.4989	0.4989	0.4989	0.4990	0.4990